SIX RED MONTHS IN RUSSIA

LOUISE BRYANT

Революціонный Комитетъ
Петроградскаго
рабочихъ и солдатскихъ
депутатовъ
Военный Отдѣлъ

2 Октября 19 г.

№ 1434

У Д О С Т О В Ѣ Р Е Н І Е 7

Настоящее удостовѣреніе дано представите-
лю Американской Соціялъ-демократіи Интернаціона-
листу товарищу Л У И З Ѣ   Б Р А Й А Н Т Ъ въ
томъ, что Военно - Революціонный Комитетъ Петер-
бургскаго Совѣта Рабочихъ и Солдатскихъ Депутатовъ предоставилъ имъ право свободнаго проѣз-
да по всему Сѣверному Фронту въ цѣляхъ освѣдом-
ленія нашихъ Американскихъ товарищей - интерна-
ціоналистовъ съ событіями въ Россіи.

Предсѣдатель:

Секретарь:

THIS PASS WAS ISSUED AT THE REQUEST OF TROTSKY SHORTLY
AFTER HE BECAME MINISTER OF FOREIGN AFFAIRS.

CERTIFICATE.—This is given to a representative of the American social democracy, an
internationalist and comrade—LOUISE BRYANT. The Military Revolutionary Committee of
the Petrograd Council of Workers' and Soldiers' Deputies gives her the right of free travel
through the entire Northern Front with the purpose of reporting to our American comrades,
internationalists, about the events in Russia.
Signed by the Secretary and Chairman.

THE REVERSE SIDE READS AS FOLLOWS :
This is a permit for free travel for the *entire Russian Front* and not only the Northern Front.
Dated Oct. 16, 1917.

FIRST PASS ISSUED BY THE MILITARY REVOLUTIONARY COMMITTEE ON THE NIGHT THAT THE BOLSHEVIKI CAME INTO POWER IN RUSSIA.

Translation:

PASS 1. Military Revolutionary of the Petrograd Council of Workers' and Soldiers' Deputies gives Tovaritche Louise Bryant free passage through the city.
Signed by the Chairman and Secretary of the
Military Revolutionary Committee.

TEN KOPECKS

TEN KOPECKS
OBVERSE

ONE KOPECK

TWO KOPECKS
Examples of Revolutionar
money—printed from old en
graved postage stamp plate

PASS TO SMOLNY. TRANSLATION: MILITARY REVOLUTIONARY COMMITTEE OF THE SOLDIERS' AND PEASANTS' DEPUTIES.

PASS No. 43. To the building of the Smolny Institute.
Tovaritche Louise Bryant,
A representative of the American Press.
Committee on Personnel—S. Peters.
December 5, 1917.

The old Breshkovsky who wishes to be ever a friend of you

KATHERINE BRESHKOVSKY
GRANDMOTHER OF THE REVOLUTION

SIX RED MONTHS IN RUSSIA

*An Observer's Account of Russia Before and
During the Proletarian Dictatorship*

BY

LOUISE BRYANT

ILLUSTRATED

The Journeyman Press
London & West Nyack

First published in the *Philadelphia Public Ledger*
between April and May 1918,
and in book form, October 1918

Reprinted by the Journeyman Press, January 1982
97 Ferme Park Road, Crouch End, London N8 9SA and
17 Old Mill Road, West Nyack, NY 10994

ISBN 0 904526 79 8

Printed in the United States of America

INTRODUCTION

I ASK a favour of him who reads this bundle of stories, gathered together on the edge of Asia, in that mystic land of white nights in summer and long black days in winter, where events only heretofore dreamed or vaguely planned for future ages have suddenly come to be. I ask the reader to remember his tolerant mood when he sits himself down under his shaded lamp of an evening to read certain lovely old legends, to remember how deliberately he gets himself out of this world into another as unlike our own as the pale moon. He should recall that in reading ancient lore he does so with an open mind, calmly, never once throwing down his book and cursing because some ancient king has marched with all his gallant warriors into another country without so much as a passport from the State Department.

We have here in America an all too obvious and objectionable prejudice against Russia. And this, you will agree, is born of fear. In Russia something strange and foreboding has occurred, it threatens to undo our present civilisation and instinctively we fear change—for better or for worse. We hug our comforts, our old habits of life, our old values. . . . There are those among us who whisper that this change will mean darkness and chaos, there are those who claim it is but a golden light which, starting from a little flame, shall circle the earth and make it glow with happiness. All that is not for me to say. I am but a messenger who lays his notes before you, attempting to give you a picture of what I saw and what you would have seen if you had been with me.

In that half year of which I write I felt as if I were continually witnessing events which might properly come some centuries later. I was continually startled and surprised. And yet I should have been prepared for surprises. All of us have felt the deep undercurrents that are turning the course of the steady tide. The great war could not leave an unchanged world in its wake—certain movements of society were bound to be pushed forward, others retarded. I speak particularly of Socialism.

Socialism is here, whether we like it or not—just as woman suffrage is here—and it spreads with the years. In Russia the socialist state is an accomplished fact. We can never again call it an idle dream of long-haired philosophers. And if that growth has resembled the sudden upshooting of a mushroom, if it must fall because it is premature, it is nevertheless real and must have tremendous effect on all that follows. Everything considered, there is just as much reason to believe that the Soviet Republic of Russia will stand as that it will fall. The most significant fact is that it will not fall from *inside* pressure. Only *outside,* foreign, hostile intervention can destroy it.

On the grey horizon of human existence looms a great giant called Working Class Consciousness. He treads with thunderous step through all the countries of the world. There is no escape, we must go out and meet him. It all depends on us whether he will turn into a loathsome, ugly monster demanding human sacrifices or whether he shall be the saviour of mankind. We must use great foresight, patience, understanding. . . . We must somehow make an honest effort to understand what is happening in Russia.

And I who saw the dawn of a new world can only present my fragmentary and scattered evidence to you with a good deal of awe. I feel as one who went forth to gather pebbles and found pearls. . . .

CONTENTS

xiii

ILLUSTRATIONS

PLATE I

GENERAL KORNILOFF
WHO HEADED THE COUNTER-REVOLUTION IN SEPTEMBER.

PLATE II

TCHEIDZE
CHAIRMAN OF THE DEMOCRATIC CONGRESS AND THE PREPARLIAMENT

PLATE III

TCHERNOFF
CHAIRMAN OF THE CONSTITUENT ASSEMBLY

PLATE IV

KERENSKY
THIS IS HIS FAVORITE PHOTOGRAPH.   HE GAVE IT TO ME WITH
HIS AUTOGRAPH A WEEK BEFORE HE WAS DEPOSED

PLATE V

*To dear comrade
Louise Bryant
from her friend
Alexandra Kollontay
Petrograd 1/9/18.*

ALEXANDRA KOLLENTAY

PLATE VI

LEON TROTSKY

ANTONOFF

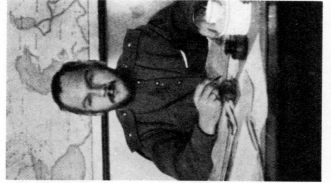

KRYLENKO

DUBENKO

PLATE VII

PLATE VIII

SPIRODONOVA
THIS IS THE ONLY PHOTOGRAPH SHE EVER GAVE TO ANYONE.   SHE
TORE IT OFF HER PASSPORT THE DAY I LEFT RUSSIA

PLATE IX

RED GUARDS ON THE STEPS OF SMOLNY

PLATE X

THE RED BURIAL HELD IN MOSCOW IN NOVEMBER
FIVE HUNDRED BODIES WERE BURIED IN ONE DAY

PLATE XI

THE REVOLUTIONARY TRIBUNAL

TO FRIENDS IN AMERICA FROM A VOLUNTEER OF THE
FIRST PETROGRAD BATTALION. "ANNA SHUB"

PLATE XII

PLATE XIII

WOMEN SOLDIERS IN FRONT OF WINTER PALACE

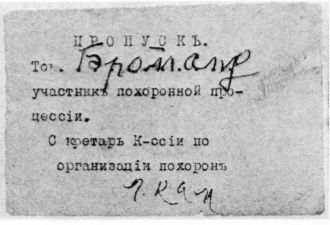

PASS
TO BRYANT
PARTICIPANT OF THE FUNERAL PROCESSION
SECRETARY OF THE ORGANIZATION
                    K. A. M.
THE SEAL READS:
MOSCOW CENTRAL EXECUTIVE COMMITTEE
COUNCIL OF SOLDIERS AND WORKERS
DEPUTIES

PASS
THE MILITARY REVOLUTIONARY COMMITTEE PERMITS LOUISE BRYANT PASSAGE FROM
PETROGRAD TO MOSCOW AND RETURN.   PASS GOOD FOR THREE DAYS FROM DATE OF ISSUANCE
DATED 8TH OF NOVEMBER, 1917
SEAL OF THE MILITARY REVOLUTIONARY COMMITTEE

PLATE XIV

PLATE XV

CROWD ON NEVSKY

SIX RED MONTHS IN RUSSIA

SIX RED MONTHS IN RUSSIA

CHAPTER I

ON THE WAY TO RUSSIA

WHEN the news of the Russian revolution flared out across the front pages of all the newspapers in the world, I made up my mind to go to Russia. I did it suddenly without thinking at all. By force of habit I put down my two pennies at a little corner newsstand and the newsdealer handed me an evening paper. There with the great city roaring around me I read the first account, a warm feeling of deep happiness spreading over me.

I had been walking with a young Russian from the East Side. Now I turned to speak to him, but he was staring at the large black letters crazily, his eyes bulging from his head. Suddenly he grabbed the paper out of my hand and ran madly through the streets. Three days later I met him —he was still embracing everybody, weeping and telling them the good news. He had spent three years in Siberia. . . .

Early in August I left America on the Danish steamer *United States*. From my elevation on

19

the first-class deck the first night out I could hear returning exiles in the steerage singing revolutionary songs. In the days that followed I spent most of my time down there; they were the only people on the boat who weren't bored to death. There were about a hundred of them, mostly Jews from the Pale. Hunted, robbed, mistreated in every conceivable manner before they fled to America, they had somehow maintained the greatest love for the land of their birth. I could not understand it then. I do now. Russia lays strong hold on the affections of even the foreign visitor.

It was a long way back to Russia for these people. We were held up in Halifax a week on their account. Every morning British officers came on board and examined and re-examined. Pitiful incidents occurred. There was an old woman who clung frantically to some letters from a dead son. She secreted them in all sorts of strange places and brought down suspicion upon herself. There was a youth they decided to detain—he threw himself face downward on the deck and sobbed loudly like a child. The whole lot of them were in a state of nervous terror; Russia was so near and yet so far. And they were held up again and again— at Christiania, at Stockholm, at Haparanda. I saw one of the men in Petrograd five months later. He had just gotten through. . . .

After we left Stockholm my own curiosity grew every hour. As our train rushed on through the vast, untouched forests of northern Sweden I could scarcely contain myself. Soon I should see how this greatest and youngest of democracies was learning to walk—to stretch itself—to feel its strength—unshackled! We were to watch that brave attempt of the new republic to establish itself with widely varying emotions, we miscellaneous folk, who were gathered together for a few hours.

The day we reached the border every one on the train was up bustling about with the first light, getting ready for the change. The rain beat mournfully against the car windows as we ate our frugal meal of sour black bread and weak coffee. Most of us had been a month on the way and we were travel-weary. We wondered vaguely what had happened in Russia—no news had leaked into Sweden since the half-credited story about the German advance on Riga.

The little ferry-boat gliding over dark, muddy waters between Haparanda and Tornea, carrying the same trainload of passengers and piled high with baggage, landed us on the edge of Finland on a cheerless grey September morning. A steady drizzle added to our discomfort. As soon as we stepped off the boat I caught my first glimpse of the Russian army; great giants of men, mostly workers and peasants, in old, dirt-coloured uniforms from which every emblem of Tsardom had been carefully removed. Brass buttons with the Imperial insignia, gold and silver epaulettes, deco-

rations, all were replaced by a simple arm-band
or a bit of red cloth. I noticed that all of them
smoked, that they did not salute and that sentries,
looking exceedingly droll, were sitting on chairs.
Military veneer seemed to have vanished. What
had taken its place?

Things began to happen as soon as we landed.
One woman in her excitement began speaking German. Then when it was discovered that her passport bore no visé from Stockholm she was hustled
roughly back over the line. She called out as she
went that she had no money, that no one had told
her she needed a visé and that she had three starving children in Russia. Her thin, hysterical voice
trailed back brokenly.

A tall, white-bearded patriarch, returning after
an enforced absence of thirty years, rushed from
one soldier to another.

"How are you, my dears? What town are you
from? How long have you been here? Ah, I am
glad to be back!"

Thus he ran on, not waiting or expecting an
answer. The soldiers smiled indulgently, although
for some mysterious reason they were in a dead-
serious mood. At length one of them made a gesture of impatience.

"Listen, Little Grandfather," he said severely
but not unkindly, "are you not aware that there
are other things to think about in Russia just now
besides family re-unions?"

The old man caught some deep significance behind his words and looked pitifully bewildered. He had been a dealer in radical books in London for many years and he had been buried in these books. He was not prepared for action; he was coming home to a millennium to die at peace in free, contented and joyful Russia. Now a premonition of fear flitted over his old face. He clutched nervously at the soldier's arm.

"What is it you have to tell me?" he cried. "Is Russia not free? What begins now but happiness and peace?"

"Now begins work," shouted several soldiers. "Now begins *more fighting and more dying!* You old ones will never understand that the job is by no means finished. Are there not enemies without and traitors within? . . ."

The old exile appeared suddenly shrunken and tired. "Tell me," he whispered, "what the trouble is."

For answer they pointed to a sign-board upon which a large, new notice was pasted and we joined an agitated little group and read:

"TO ALL-ALL-ALL:

"On the 26th of August (September 8th, our time) General Korniloff despatched to me, Duma member V. N. Lvov, with a demand to give him over supreme military and civilian power, saying that he will form a new government to rule the country. I verified the authority of this Duma member by direct telephonic communication with General Korniloff. I saw in this demand addressed to the Provisional Government the desire of a certain class of the Russian people to take advantage of the desperate situation of our nation, to reestablish that system of order which would be in contradiction to the acquisition of our Revolution; and therefore the Provisional Government considered it necessary for the salvation of the country, of liberty and democratic government, to take all measures to secure order in the country and by any means suppress all attempts to usurp the supreme power in the State and to usurp the rights won by our citizens in the Revolution. These measures I put into operation and will inform the Nation more fully of them. At the same time, I ordered General Korniloff to hand over the command to General Klembovsky, Commander-in-Chief of the Northern Front, defending the way to Petrograd. And herewith I appoint General Klembovsky Commander-in-Chief of all the Russian Armies. The City of Petrograd and the Petrograd District is declared under martial law by action of this telegram. I appeal to all citizens that they should conserve the peace and order so neces-

sary for the salvation of the country and to
all the officers of the army and fleet I appeal
to accomplish their duties in defending the
Nation from the external enemy.

"(Signed)   PREMIER KERENSKY."

So I had arrived on the crest of a *counter-
revolution!* Korniloff was marching on Petrograd.
Petrograd was in a state of siege.   Trenches were
at that very moment being dug outside the city.
The telegram from Kerensky was two days old.
What had happened since then?   Wild rumour followed wild rumour.   In fact, such exaggeration
abounded that the whole outlook of the country
was completely changed in each overheated report.
We walked up and down the station under heavy
guard, like prisoners. . . .

Everything was in confusion; passports and luggage were examined over and over.   I was marched
into a small, cold, badly lit room, guarded by six
soldiers with long, business-like looking bayonets.
In the room was a stocky Russian girl.   She mo-
tioned for me to remove my clothes.   This I did,
wondering.   Once they were off she ordered me
to put them on again without any examination.   I
was curious.   "It's just a rule," she said, smiling at
my incomprehension.

There were British officers here and they advised
me not to proceed.   "The Germans have taken
Riga and are already across the Dvina; when they

get to Petrograd they will cut you in pieces!"
With such gloomy predictions I left the frontier
town and sped onward through flat, monotonous
Finland. . . .

CHAPTER II

NOBODY believed that our train would ever really reach Petrograd. In case it was stopped I had made up my mind to walk, so I was extremely grateful for every mile that we covered. It was a ridiculous journey, more like something out of an extravagant play than anything in real life.

Next to my compartment was a General, super-refined, painfully neat, with waxed moustachios. There were several monarchists, a diplomatic courier, three aviators of uncertain political opinion and, further along, a number of political exiles who had been held up in Sweden for a month and were the last to return at the expense of the new government. Rough, almost ragged soldiers climbed aboard continually, looked us over and departed. Often they hesitated before the General's door and regarded him suspiciously, never at any time did they honour him with the slightest military courtesy. He sat rigid in his seat and stared back at them coldly. Every one was too agitated to be silent or even discreet. At every station we all dashed out to enquire the news and buy papers.

At one place we were informed that the Cossacks were all with Korniloff as well as the artillery; the people were helpless. At this alarming news the monarchists began to assert themselves. They confided to me in just what manner they thought the revolutionary leaders ought to be publicly tortured and finally given death sentences.

The next rumour had it that Kerensky had been murdered and all Russia was in a panic; in Petrograd the streets were running blood. The returning exiles looked pale and wretched. So this then was their joyful home-coming! They sighed but they were exceedingly brave. "Ah, well, we will fight it all over again!" they said with marvellous determination. I made no comments. I was conscious of an odd sense of loneliness; I was an alien in a strange land.

At all the stations soldiers were gathered in little knots of six and seven; talking, arguing, gesticulating. Once a big, bewhiskered *mujik* thrust his head in at a car window, pointed menacingly at a well-dressed passenger and bellowed interrogatively, *"Burzhouee!"* (Bourgeoise). He looked very comical, yet no one laughed. . . .

We had become so excited we could scarcely keep our seats. We crowded into the narrow corridor, peering out at the desolate country, reading our papers and conjecturing . . .

All this confusion seemed to whet our appetites. At Helsingfors we saw heaping dishes of food in the railway restaurant. A boy at the door explained the procedure: first we must buy little tickets and then we could eat as much as we pleased. To our astonishment the cashier refused the Russian money which we had so carefully obtained before leaving Sweden.

"But this is ridiculous!" I told the cashier. "Finland is part of Russia! Why shouldn't you take this money?"

Flames shot up in her eyes. "It will not long be a part of Russia!" she snapped. "Finland shall be a republic!" Here was a brand new situation. How fast they came now, these complications.

Feeling utterly at a loss, we strolled up and down, complaining bitterly. Once we found we could not buy food, our hunger grew alarmingly. We were saved by a passenger from another car who had plenty of Finnish marks and was willing to take our rubles.

At Wiborg we felt the tension was deep and ominous. We were suddenly afraid to enquire the news of the crowds on the platform. There were literally hundreds of soldiers, their faces haggard, in the half light of late afternoon. The scraps of conversation we caught sent shivers over us.

"All the generals ought to be killed!" "We must rid ourselves of the bourgeoisie!" "No, that is not right." "I am not in favour of that!" "All killing is wrong. . . ."

A pale, slight youth, standing close beside me, unexpectedly blurted out in a sort of stage whisper, "It was terrible. . . . I heard them screaming!"

I questioned him anxiously. "Heard who? Heard who?"

"The officers! The bright, pretty officers! They stamped on their faces with heavy boots, dragged them through the mud . . . threw them in the canal." He looked up and down fearfully, his words coming in jerks. "They have just finished it now," he said, still whispering, "they have killed fifty, and I have heard them screaming."

Once the train moved again we pieced together our fragments of news and made out the following story:

Early the day before had arrived messages from Kerensky, ordering the troops to Petrograd to defend the city. The officers had received the messages but remained silent and gave no orders. The soldiers had grown suspicious. They mumbled together and their mumblings had become a roar. At some one's suggestion, they marched in a body and searched for the messages. The messages were found. Their worst suspicions were confirmed. Rage and revenge swept them away. They did not stop to separate innocent from guilty. The officers were sympathisers of Korniloff, they were aristocrats, they were enemies of the revolution! In quick, wild anger they dealt out terrible punishment.

The details of the massacre were exceedingly ugly, but no description of mine is necessary. Every Russian writer who has ever written about mob violence has described the swift terribleness of these scenes with amazing frankness. Realising that the most serious of all dissolution and revolt is military mutiny, our hearts fluttered at the unutterable possibilities. . . .

We were interrupted in our reflections by a wail from the Russian courier who found himself in a curious dilemma. "What shall I do?" he asked of us dismally. "I have been nearly a month at sea and God knows what has happened to my unfortunate country in that time. God knows what is happening now. If I deliver my papers to the wrong faction it will be fatal!"

It was past midnight when we stopped at Beeloostrov. It was the last station. We were so certain all along that we would never get to Petrograd that we were not surprised now when soldiers came on board and ordered us all out. We soon found, however, that it was just another tiresome examination. Crowded into a great bare room, we stood shivering nervously while our baggage was hurled pell-mell into another. As our names were called we submitted our passports, answered questions, wrote down our nationality, our religion, our purpose in Russia, and hurried to unlock our trunks for the impatient soldiers.

The officers startled us by beginning to confiscate all sorts of ordinary things. We protested as much as we dared. In explanation they replied that a new order had just come in prohibiting medicines, cosmetics and what-not.

Next to me in line was an indignant princess whose luggage contained many precious "aids to beauty," all of which had already been passed hurriedly by bashful censors and custom officials many times before. But that unreasonable new order upset everything; rouge-sticks followed rare perfumes, French powder, brilliantine, hair-dye—all were thrown roughly into a great unpainted box, a box whose contents grew rapidly higher and higher, a box that had the magic power to change what was *art* in one's hand-bag into *rubbish* in its insatiable maw.

The princess pleaded with the soldiers, used feminine wiles, burst into hysterical weeping. Poor, unhappy princess, forty, with a flirtatious husband, handsome and twenty-three! The situation was far too subtle for these crude defenders of the revolution! Only an old monarchist dared to be sympathetic, but I noted that he took care to be sympathetic in English, a language few of his countrymen understand.

"Madame," he remarked testily, "there is a strong hint of stupid morality in all this. You

must remember that to the uncultured all implements of refinement are considered immoral!"

The husband offered tardy consolation. "Be
calm, my darling, you shall have all these things
again." Unfortunately he would never be able
to make good his promise, for in these rough days
of the new order cosmetics are not considered important and Russian ladies are forced to go "au
natural."

We arrived in Petrograd at three in the morning prepared for anything but the apparent order
and the deep enveloping stillness that comes before dawn. My friends of the train soon scattered and were lost in the night, and I stood there
in the great station confused, with what was left
of my baggage.

Presently a young soldier came running. *"Aft-
mobile?"* he enquired in a honeyed voice. *"Aftmo-
bile?"* I nodded assent, not knowing what else to
do and in a moment we were outside before a big
grey car. In the car was another soldier, also
young and pleasant. I gave them the name of a
hotel some one had told me about—the Angleterre.

So we were off whirling through the deserted
streets. Here and there we encountered sentries
who called out sharply, received the proper word,
and allowed us to pass. I was consumed with
curiosity. These soldiers wore neither arm-bands
nor bits of ribbon. I had no way of knowing who
or what they were . . . One of them wanted to be

entertaining, so he began to tell me about the first days of the revolution and how wonderful it was.

"The crowd raised a man on their shoulders," he said, "when they saw the Cossacks coming. And the man shouted, 'If you have come to destroy the revolution, shoot me first,' and the Cossacks replied, 'We do not shoot our brothers.' Some of the old people who remembered how long the Cossacks had been our enemies almost went mad with joy."

He ceased speaking. Mysteriously out of the darkness the bells in all the churches began to boom over the sleeping city, a sort of wild barbaric tango of bells, like nothing else I had ever heard. . . .

CHAPTER III

THE sleepy porter of the Hotel Angleterre fumbled his keys and finally got the door open. My two soldiers rode away waving their hands cheerfully; I never saw them again. The porter took my passport and put it in the safe without looking at it and shuffled along upstairs ahead of me until we reached a large vault-like suite on the third floor.

It was four o'clock and not for many hours would it be light—Petrograd is very far north to a New Yorker. By December when things had reached such a desperate state that we seldom had artificial light at all, because there was no coal to run the power plants, we seemed to live in perpetual darkness. I have often purchased, in the deserted churches, holy candles which were designated to be burned before the shrines of saints but which were carried home surreptitiously in order to see to write. But in October the lights were still running. When the porter pressed the button I blinked painfully under the dazzling blaze of sparkling old-fashioned crystal candelabra.

I looked around at the great unfriendly room in which I found myself. It was all gold and mahogany with old blue draperies; most of the furniture was still wearing its summer garments. I had a feeling that no one had lived in this room for years—it had a musty, unused smell. Lost in a remote corner of the room adjoining was my bed and beyond that an enormous bath-tub, cut out of solid granite, coldly reflected the light.

For all this elegance? "Thirty rubles," the porter murmured, still half awake.

There was a large sign above my bed forbidding me to speak German—the penalty being fifteen hundred rubles. I had no desire to break the law. It seemed a lot to pay for so small amount of enjoyment, I thought as I slid bravely down between the icy sheets and fell into a dead slumber.

I was awakened by loud knocks on my door. A burly Russian entered and began to bellow about my baggage. I rubbed my eyes and tried to make out what language he was speaking and suddenly I realised—he was speaking German! I pointed to the sign and he shook with laughter.

I found out afterwards that no one pays any attention to signs in Russia. They read the signs and then use their own judgment. Take language, for instance. Few foreigners ever learn to speak Russian; on the other hand, they are very apt to have at least a smattering of French or German. Solution: speak the language you understand. If

you tell them German is an enemy language they
will tell you that they are not at war with the language. Furthermore, they have found their use of
it very valuable in getting over propaganda into
Austria and Germany.

Just across from my window, St. Isaac's Cathedral loomed blackly and I watched the bellringers
in the ponderous cupolas, bell-ropes tied to elbows,
knees, feet and hands, making the maddest music
with great and little bells. The people passing
looked up also and occasionally one crossed himself.

Out on the streets I wandered aimlessly noting
the contents of the little shops now pitifully empty.
It is curious the things that remain in a starving
and besieged city. There was only food enough to
last three days, there were no warm clothes at all
and I passed window after window full of flowers,
corsets, dog-collars and false hair!

This absurd combination can be accounted for
without much scientific investigation. The corsets
were of the most expensive, out-of-date, wasp-
waist variety and the women who wear them have
largely disappeared from the capital.

The reason for the false hair and dog collars was
equally plain. About a third of the women of
the towns wear their hair short and there is no market for the tons of beautiful hair in the shops,
marked down to a few rubles. An enterprising
dealer in such goods could make a fortune by ex-

porting the gold, brown and auburn tresses of the shorn and emancipated female population of Russia and selling them in America, France or some other backward country where women still cling to hairpins.

As for the dog collars, just imagine any one being a dog-fancier or even a fondler of dogs to the extent of purchasing a gold-rimmed or a diamond-studded collar while a Revolutionary Tribunal is sitting just around the corner. Whatever class lines there were among dogs fell with the Tsar.

And the masses of flowers. Horticulture had reached a high state of development before the revolution. This was especially true of exotic flowers because of the extravagant tastes of the upper classes. With the change in government the demand for these luxuries abruptly ceased; but there were still the hot-houses, there were still the old gardeners. It is impossible to break off old-established things in the twinkling of an eye. Habits of trade are as hard to break as any other habits of life. So the shops continued to be filled with flowers. On the Morskaya where so much bitter street fighting occurred were three flower-shops —in them were displayed always the rarest varieties of orchids. And in those turbulent January days suddenly appeared—white lilacs!

These strange left-overs of another time cropped up everywhere making sharp contrasts. There were the men, for instance, who stood outside of the

palaces and the big hotels, peacock feathers in their
round Chinese-looking caps and wearing green,
gold or scarlet sashes. Their duty had been to as-
sist people who alighted from carriages, but now
grand personages never arrived, and still they stood
there, their sashes bedraggled and faded, their
feathers ragged and forlorn. As helpless they were
as the old negroes of the South who clung to their
slavery after the emancipation.

And in contrast were the waiters bustling about
in the restaurants inside of the very buildings
where the *svetzars* stood before the doors like
courtiers without a court. They ran their restaurants co-operatively and at every table was a
curt little notice.

"Just because a man must make his living by
being a waiter do not insult him by offering him a
tip."

Petrograd is impressive, vast and solid. New
York's high buildings have a sort of tall flimsiness
about them that is not sinister; Petrograd looks
as if it were built by a giant who had no regard for
human life. The rugged strength of Peter the
Great is in all the broad streets, the mighty open
spaces, the great canals curving through the city,
the rows and rows of palaces and the immense fa-
çades of government buildings. Even such exquisite bits of architecture as the graceful gold
spires of the old Admiralty building and the round

blue-green domes of the Turquoise Mosque, cannot break that heaviness. . . .

Built by the cruel wilfulness of an autocrat, over the bodies of thousands of slaves, against the unanimous will of all grades of society, this huge artificial city, by a peculiar irony has become the heart of world revolution; has become *Red Petrograd!*

There were wonderful tales about the defeat of Korniloff and what they described as a "new kind of fighting." Every one was anxious to tell his version of how the scouts went out and met the army of the counter-revolutionists and fraternised with them and overcame them "with talk" so that they refused to fight and turned against their leaders. There was little variation, in short, the story was this:

The scouts came upon the hostile army encamped for the night and went among them saying: "Why have you come to destroy the revolution?" The hostile army indignantly denied the charge, claiming that they had been sent to "save" the revolution. So the scouts continued to argue. "Do not believe the lies your leaders tell you. We are both fighting for the same thing. Come to Petrograd with us and sit in our councils, learn the truth, and you will abandon this Korniloff who is attempting to betray you."

Accordingly delegates were sent to Petrograd. When they reported to their regiments the two armies joined as brothers.

While all this fraternising was going on and no one was sure of its results, revolutionists in Petrograd worked feverishly. In one place they told me that they had manufactured a whole cannon in thirty hours and the trenches that encircled the city were dug over night.

Ugly tales went round about the fall of Riga. Most Russians, with fairly good reason, believe that it was sold out. It fell just after General Korniloff said in public: "Must we pay with Riga the price of bringing the country to its senses?"

No one ever explained the reason for the vague order given to the retreating Russian army: *"Go north and turn to the left!"* Bewildered soldiers retreated in confusion for days without officers or further instructions, finally entrenching themselves, forming Soldiers' Committees, beginning to fight again. . . .

Officers returning a week or two afterwards told an amazing story. It was printed in the conservative paper *Vetcherneie Vremya* and I heard it twice myself from men who were captured, and I believe it to be true. When Riga fell many prisoners were taken. It was towards the end of the week. On Sunday there were services at which the Kaiser appeared and made a speech to the Russian soldiers. He called them "dogs" and berated them for killing their officers whom he claimed were brave and admirable gentlemen, commanding his respect. Consistent with Prussian military ideals, he made a practical demonstration by allowing the officers full freedom and issuing orders that the common soldiers should have little food and hard work and in certain cases a flogging. The hundreds of thousands of tubercular Russian prisoners now returning to Russia are evidence of how well the instructions were carried out. In his speech to the soldiers in the church the Kaiser said: "Pray for the government of Alexander III., not for your present disgraceful government."

That evening he dined the officers and they came back into Russia and explained that we did not "understand" the Kaiser. . . .

In Petrograd one of the things that strike coldness to one's heart are the long lines of scantily clad people standing in the bitter cold waiting to buy bread, milk, sugar or tobacco. From four o'clock in the morning they begin to stand there, while it is still black night. Often after standing in line for hours the supplies run out. Most of the time only one-fourth pound of bread for two days was allowed; and the soggy black peasant's bread is the staff of life in Russia—it is not a "trimming" like our American bread. Cabbage is also a staple diet.

On my second night in Petrograd I met a Russian from New York. We strolled up and down the Nevsky Prospect. All Russia promenades the Nevsky; it is one of the great streets of the world. My friend wanted to be hospitable as all Russians are, but he was very poor. We passed a little booth

and spied a few bars of American chocolate—5c
bars. He enquired the price—*seven rubles!* With
true Russian recklessness he paid out his last
kopeck and said: "Come, let us walk up and down
once again, it is only a mile. . . ."

Petrograd with food for three days was not
tragic or sad. Russians accept hardships uncom-
plainingly. When I first went there I was in-
clined to put it down to servility, but now I believe it to be because they have unconquerable spirit. Weeks at a stretch the street cars would not
run. People walked great distances without a
murmur and the life of the city went on as usual.
It would have upset New York completely, especially if it happened as it did in Petrograd that
while the street cars were stopped, lights and water
also were turned off and it was almost impossible
to get fuel to keep warm.

The most remarkable thing about Russians is
this wonderful persistence. Theatres somehow
managed to run two or three times a week. The
Nevsky after midnight was as amusing and interesting as Fifth Avenue in the afternoon. The
cafés had nothing to serve but weak tea and sandwiches but they were always full. A wide range
of costumes made the picture infinitely more interesting. There is practically no "fashion" in
Russia. Men and women wear what they please.
At one table would be sitting a soldier with his
fur hat pulled over one ear, across from him a Red

Guard in rag-tags, next a Cossack in a gold and black uniform, earrings in his ears, silver chains around his neck, or a man from the Wild Division, recruited from one of the most savage tribes of the Caucasus, wearing his sombre, flowing cape. . . .

And the girls that frequented these places were by no means all prostitutes, although they talked to everybody. Prostitution as an institution has not been recognised since the first revolution. The degrading "Yellow Tickets" were destroyed and many of the women became nurses and went to the front or sought other legal employment. Russian women are peculiar in regard to dress. If they are interested in revolution, they almost invariably refuse to think of dress at all and go about looking noticeably shabby—if they are not interested they care exceedingly for clothes and manage to array themselves in the most fantastic "inspirations."

I shall always remember Karsavina, the most beautiful dancer in the world, in those meagre days, dancing to a packed house. It was a marvellous audience; an audience in rags; an audience that had gone without bread to buy the cheap little tickets. I think Karsavina must have wondered what it would be like to dance before that tired, undernourished crowd instead of her once glittering and exclusive little band of nobles.

When she came on it was as hushed as death. And how she danced and how they followed her! Russians know dancing as the Italians know their

operas; every little beautiful trick they appreciate
to the utmost. "Bravo! Bravo!" roared ten thousand throats. And when she had finished they could
not let her go—again and again and again she had
to come back until she was wilted like a tired but-
terfly. Twenty, thirty times she returned, bowing, smiling, pirouetting, until we lost count. . . .
Then the people filed out into the damp winter
night, pulling their thin cloaks about them.

In Petrograd were flags—all red. Even the
statue of Catherine the Great in the little square
before the Alexandrinsky Theatre did not escape.
There stood Catherine with all her favourite courtiers sitting at her feet and on Catherine's sceptre
waved a red flag! These little visible signs of the
revolution were everywhere. Great blotches
marked the places where imperial insignia had been
torn from the buildings. Mild mannered guards
patrolled the principal corners, trying not to offend
anybody. And over it all stalked King Hunger
while a chill autumn rain soaked into the half-fed
shivering throngs that hurried along, lifting their
faces and beholding a vision of world democracy. . . .

CHAPTER IV

SMOLNY INSTITUTE, headquarters of the Bolsheviki, is on the edge of Petrograd. Years ago it was considered "way out in the country," but the city grew out to meet it, engulfed it and finally claimed it as its own. Smolny is an enormous place; the great main building stretches in a straight line for hundreds of feet with an ell jutting out at each end and forming a sort of elongated court. Close up to the north ell snuggles the lovely little Smolny Convent with its dull blue domes with the silver stars. Once young ladies of noble birth from all over Russia came here to receive a "proper" education.

I came to know Smolny well while I was in Russia. I saw it change from a lonely, deserted barracks into a busy humming hive, heart and soul of the last revolution. I watched the leaders once accused, hunted and imprisoned raised by the mass of the people of all Russia to the highest places in the nation. They were borne along on the whirlwind of radicalism that swept and is still sweeping Russia and they themselves did not know how

long or how well they would be able to ride that
whirlwind. . . .

Smolny was always a strange place. In the cav-
ernous, dark hallways where here and there flick-
ered a pale electric light, thousands and thousands
of soldiers and sailors and factory workers tramped
in their heavy, mud-covered boots every day. All
the world seemed to have business at Smolny and
the polished white floors over which once tripped
the light feet of careless young ladies became dark
and dirt-stained and the great building shook with
the tread of the proletariat. . . .

I ate many of my meals in the great mess hall
on the ground floor with the soldiers. There were
long, rough wooden tables and wooden benches and
a great air of friendliness pervaded everywhere.
You were always welcome at Smolny if you were
poor and you were hungry. We ate with wooden
spoons, the kind the Russian soldiers carry in their
big boots, and all we had to eat was cabbage soup
and black bread. We were always thankful for
it and always afraid that perhaps to-morrow
there would not be even that. . . . We stood in long
lines at the noon hour chattering like children. "So
you are an American, Tavarishe, well, how does it
go now in America?" they would say to me.

Upstairs in a little room tea was served night
and day. Trotsky used to come there and Kollontay and Spiradonova and Kaminoff and Volo-
darysky and all the rest except Lenine. I never saw

Lenine at either of these places. He held aloof and only appeared at the largest meetings and no one got to know him very well. But the others I mentioned would discuss events with us. In fact, they were very generous about giving out news.

In all the former classrooms typewriters ticked incessantly. Smolny worked twenty-four hours a day. For weeks Trotsky never left the building. He ate and slept and worked in his office on the third floor and strings of people came in every hour of the day to see him. All the leaders were frightfully overworked, they looked haggard and pale from loss of sleep.

In the great white hall, once the ball-room, with its graceful columns and silver candelabra, delegates from the Soviets all over Russia met in all-night sessions. Men came straight from the first line trenches, straight from the fields and the factories. Every race in Russia met there as brothers. Men poured out their souls at these meetings and they said beautiful and terrible things. I will give you an example of the speeches of the soldiers:

A tired, emaciated little soldier mounts the rostrum. He is covered with mud from head to foot and with old blood stains. He blinks in the glaring light. It is the first speech he has ever made in his life and he begins it in a shrill hysterical shout:

"Tavarishi! I come from the place where men are digging their graves and calling them trenches!

We are forgotten out there in the snow and the cold. *We are forgotten while you sit here and discuss politics!* I tell you the army can't fight much longer! *Something's got to be done! Something's got to be done!* The officers won't work with the soldiers' committees and the soldiers are starving and the Allies won't have a conference. *I tell you something's got to be done or the soldiers are going home!"*

Then the peasants would get up and plead for their land. The Land Committees, they claimed, were being arrested by the Provisional Government; they had a religious feeling about land. They said they would fight and die for the land, but they would not wait any longer. *If it was not given to them now they would go out and take it.*

And the factory workers told of the sabotage of the bourgeoisie, how they were ruining the delicate machinery so that the workmen could not run the factories; they were shutting down the mills so they would starve. It was not true, they cried, that the workers were getting fabulous sums. *They couldn't live on what they got!*

Over and over and over like the beat of the surf came the cry of all starving Russia: *"Peace, land and bread!"*

It would be very unjust to blame the leaders for any steps they took, my observation was that they were always pushed into these actions by the great will of the majority. It is certainly

foolish also to think that the peasants were iso-
lated from Smolny. One of the most spectacular
events that happened in Petrograd after the revolution was the two-mile parade of peasants from
6 Fontanka, where they were having the meeting
of the All-Russian Peasants' Congress, to Smolny,
just to show their approval of that institution.

So many different organisations had offices in
Smolny. There worked the now famous Military
Revolutionary Committee in Room 17, on the top
floor. This committee, which performed some extraordinary feats during the first days of the Bolshevik uprising, was headed by Lazarimov, an
eighteen-year-old boy. It was a throbbing room;
couriers came and went, foreigners stood in line to
get passes to leave the country, suspects were
brought in. . . .

Antonoff, the War Minister, had an office in
Smolny, as well as Krylenko and Dubenko, so it
was the nerve centre for the army and navy, as well
as the political centre.

In the corridors were stacks of literature which
the people gobbled up eagerly. Pamphlets, books
and official newspapers of the Bolshevik party like
Rabotchi Poot and the *Isvestia* by the thousands
were disposed of daily.

Soldiers, dead-weary, slept in the halls and on
chairs and benches in unused rooms. Others stood
alert and on guard before all sorts of committee
rooms, and if you didn't have a pass like the one

reproduced in this book you didn't get in. The
passes were changed frequently to keep out spies.

In many windows were machine guns pointing
blind eyes into the cold winter air. Rifles were
stacked along the walls, and on the stone steps before the main entrance were several cannon. In
the court were armoured cars ready for action.
Smolny was always well guarded by volunteers.

No matter how late the meetings lasted, and they
usually broke up about 4 o'clock in the morning,
the street-car employees kept the cars waiting.
When the heaviest snowstorms blocked up the traf-
fic, soldiers and sailors and working women came
out on the streets and kept the tracks clear to
Smolny. Often it was the only line running in the
city.

I have heard that Smolny was the bought estab-
lishment of the German imperialists. I have tried
to give a true picture of Smolny. It was not the
kind of place in which an imperialist of any sort
would have been comfortable. I never heard any
leader or any of the thousands of soldiers, workers
or peasants who came there express one trace of
sympathy for the German Government. They
have, however, the same feeling that President Wilson has about speaking to the people of Austria
and Germany over the heads of their autocratic
military leaders. And how successful they are in
this must one day be obvious to a doubting world.

CHAPTER V

EXPLANATION OF POLITICAL PARTIES

EVERY change or development of the political
situation in Russia will appear vague and in-
comprehensible unless one understands the essential points of the various political parties and has
some definite idea of the way a Soviet government
works.   In order to do so it is not at all necessary
to go into the fine points of Socialism, which the
average reader probably has neither time nor in-
clination for, but just to get a broad general idea.
In writing this I do not write as a Socialist, but as
a layman speaking to laymen.   I attempt to give
no pointers to students of political economy. They
will be familiar with this outline and much more.

The first thing to remember is that *all the important political parties in Russia are Socialist
parties—except the Cadets.*

The Cadet party is the party of the propertied
classes; it has no force of arms and no great mass
of people.   At one time the only accredited legal
party which stood for fairness and reform, as the
revolution progressed it lost in influence and fell
rapidly into ill repute.

Marie Spirodonova, in speaking of the Cadets,

RUSSIAN POLITICAL PARTIES

Parties	Monarchists and reactionary parties which disappeared at beginning of Rev. Later these elements entered Cadet party	Cadets	Mensheviki, Socialist Revolutionaries and other moderate Socialist groups	Bolsheviki and Left Socialist Revolutionaries
Classes represented	Feudal land-owners, reactionary capitalists	Liberal land owners, liberal capitalists, professional classes	Socialist intellectuals, proprietors, well-to-do peasants	Industrial workers, day labourers, poor peasants
Attitude towards Socialism	Unconditionally hostile	Unconditionally hostile	For Socialism but consider this not the time for realisation	For Socialism through a proletarian dictatorship
Form of government	Autocracy	Bourgeois parliamentary republic or Constitutional monarchy like England	Parliamentary Republic based on coalition of Socialists and bourgeois classes	Republic based on Soviets of Soldiers', Workers' and Peasants' Deputies
Attitude toward the war	Coalition of autocracies and Great Russia	Russia a great power in alliance with Allies. Wanted Dardanelles and expansion in Asia Minor	Wanted peace but no break with Allies	Immediate general democratic peace. Hostile to Germany but also not in sympathy with alleged imperialistic war aims of other belligerents

said: "It is impossible at the present moment to be anything more reactionary than a Cadet. The reason is simple. No one dares to come out openly in favour of a monarchy or to say he is hostile to Socialism, so naturally all these people hide behind the Cadet party—claim to be Cadets, although they are not actually members and they do their best to destroy it. That is why the party that was once an honest, liberal party has become the Black Hundred organisation—hated and despised."

Katherine Breshkovsky, in one of her speeches, expressed much the same opinion. "As regards our capitalists, great and small, I must tell you that upon them rests a great, bloody sin. I am impartial—you know the class I come from—I repeat our enemy at home is just this merchant and capitalist class."

In trying to compare the deep chasm between the mass of the people in Russia and our own people where lines are hardly discernible, we must remember that in Russia over 80 per cent. of the people are proletariat or semi-proletariat. That is, they are either entirely without property or they have such small holdings that they are unable to exist from them. On the other hand—after the revolution the propertied classes refused to co-operate in any way with the democratic organisations of the masses. They bent every effort to break down those institutions.

Often our press speaks of the Socialist Revolutionists or the Mensheviki as if they were "reasonable" and conservative parties as opposed to the radical Bolsheviki. They commonly speak of the Bolsheviki as Anarchists and as Maximalists. All these ideas are far from correct. *The Mensheviki and the Bolsheviki are branches of the same party* and until 1903 they worked together. They still have precisely the same programme, but they differ as to tactics. They are both Social Democrats —Marxians. They got their names because of the split. The majority of the party went with the Bolsheviki and the minority went with the Mensheviki. That is what their names mean—*majori-*

tists and *minoritists.* Both stand for the socialization of the industry and the land. They differ in
tactics.

In October, 1917, the Bolsheviki accepted the
Socialist Revolutionists' land programme. This
was to provisionally divide the land but at the same
time to abolish all private ownership of land.

The Socialist Revolutionists—the party of the
peasants—is by far the greatest party in Russia.
In 1917 this party also split. It is now divided
into two groups known as the Socialist Revolutionists and the Left Socialist Revolutionists—
representing the conservative and the radical wings.

The right wing of the Socialist Revolutionists
and the Mensheviki—like the Cadets—have at present no following and no force of arms. The active
masses have gone to the left wing of the Socialist
Revolutionists which works with the Bolsheviki and
upholds the Soviet Government.

This moving of the masses away from the moderate groups is largely due to the policy of a government composed of Socialists and bourgeoisie
which led to a denial of the desires of the Russian
masses—peace, land and control of industry.

In a modern revolution all middle parties dis-
appear or become unimportant. In Russia, where
the proletariat is armed, the proletariat becomes
the only real influential body. *The Bolsheviki are
in power because they bow to the will of the masses.*

The Bolsheviki would be overthrown the very moment they did not express that will.

There are other small Socialist groups in Russia—namely, the Mensheviki Internationalists, a branch of the Menshevik party; Iedinstvo, Plechanov's party, the extreme war party of the Mensheviki; Troudoviki or Populist Socialists, a semi-Socialist party; United Social Democrat Internationalists (Gorki's party), etc.

The Maximalists are a small group—an offshoot of the Socialist Revolutionist party. Their programme is practically agrarian Anarchism.

That the Bolsheviki are not Anarchists but Socialists with a political instead of an entirely economic programme is best demonstrated by the fact that they opposed the attempted irresponsible confiscation of property by the Anarchists *with force of arms.*

The Soviet Government

The Soviets were such a natural form of organisation for the Russian masses to take because of their long experience with primitive communistic institutions. They owe their strong hold on the people to the fact that they are the most democratic and sensitive political organs that have ever been invented.

The Soviet is an organ of direct proportional representation based on small units of the popula-

tion with one representative to every 500. It is
elected by equal suffrage, secret ballot, with full
right of recall. A Soviet is not elected at regular
periods. The separate delegates, however, can be
recalled and re-elected by their constituents at any
time. Therefore, the complexion of the Soviet immediately registers the feeling of the masses of the
population. Soviets are based directly on the workers in the factories, the soldiers in the trenches and
the peasants in the fields.

Every town has a joint *Soviet of Soldiers' and
Workers' Deputies.* The different wards of the
towns also have soviets. Provinces, counties and
some villages have *Peasants' Soviets.* The *All-
Russian Congress of Soviets* is made up of delegates from the provincial soviets, which also may
be directly elected, the proportion being one delegate to each 25,000.

The *All-Russian Soviet* usually meets about
every three months. It elects a *Central Executive Committee* which is the *Parliament of the
Country.* The Central Executive Committee con-
sists of nearly 300 members. The *People's Commissars which are the Cabinet* or *Ministry,* of which
Trotsky is one, Lunarcharsky another, and so on,
are elected by the Central Executive Committee.
The Commissars are simply men at the head of a
collegium for every department of the government.
Lenine is the chairman of the Commissars.

The whole purpose of the Soviets is not simply

a territorial representation, but also a class body—
a body representing one class mainly—the working
class.

*The Soviets are the only organised force in Rus-
sia that is definitely anti-German.* No further
explanation is necessary than to say that they are
opposed on every point and the two governments
cannot exist side by side.

*Another important point to remember is that
both the Provisional Governments existed only so
long as they were tolerated by the Soviets.*

CHAPTER VI

THE DEMOCRATIC CONGRESS

WHEN the counter-revolution, headed by
General Korniloff, was at its height and
Russia, bewildered by internal and external
enemies, rushed frantically this way and that and
in her confusion allowed the fall of Riga, the
Executive Committee of the All-Russian Soviets
demanded the holding of a Democratic Congress,
which was to be a fore-runner of the Constituent
Assembly and was to make further counter-revolution impossible.

Accordingly about a month later 1600 delegates
from all parts of Russia answered the summons. It
was a cold mid-September evening, and the rain
glistened on the pavements and splashed down from
the great statue of Catherine in the leafy little
square before the entrance of the Alexandrinsky
Theatre, as the delegates filed past the long lines of
soldiers, solemnly presented their cards and disappeared into the brilliantly lighted interior of the
immense building.

Our little army of reporters, of which about six
spoke English, went around to the stage door at

the back, climbed up many dark stairs, down many more, tip-toed behind the wings and finally emerged into the orchestra pit, where places were arranged for us.

On the stage sat the presidium at long tables, behind them the entire Petrograd Soviet and in the main theatre and galleries sat the delegates. Almost every revolutionary leader was present, and there were representatives from the All-Russian Soviets of Soldiers and Workmen, the All-Russian Soviets of Peasants, Provisional Delegates of the Soldiers and Workmen's Soviets, Delegates of the Peasants' Regional Soviets, Labor Unions, Army Committees at the Front, Workmen's and Peasants' Co-operatives, Railroad Employees, Postal and Telegraph Employees, Commercial Employees, Liberal Professions (doctors, lawyers, etc.), Zemstvos, Cossacks, Press, and Nationalist Organisations, including Ukranians, Poles, Jews, Letts, Lithuanians, etc. No body just like it had ever met in Russia before.

The boxes which were formerly retained exclusively for members of the Tsar's family, were filled with foreign diplomats and other distinguished visitors. Hanging from these boxes were flaming revolutionary banners. The royal arms and other imperial insignia had been torn from the walls, leaving startling grey patches in the rich gold, ivory and crimson colour scheme. We scarcely had time to glance about before the Congress was formally

opened by President Tcheidze, and Kerensky came
forward to make his address. All day rumours had
been flying about Petrograd that he would not be
present and that he disapproved of the Congress.
One felt all over the house the suppressed excitement created by his appearance.

Only persons of great intensity can make an audience hold its breath in just the way Kerensky did
as he walked quickly across the stage. He was
clad in a plain brown soldier's suit without so much
as a brass button or an epaulette to mark him Commander-in-Chief of the Russian Army and Navy
and Minister-President of the Russian Republic.
Somehow all this unpretentiousness accentuated
the dignity of his position. It was characteristic
that he should ignore the speakers' rostrum and proceed to the runway leading from the main floor to
the stage. It produced an effect of unusual in-
timacy between the speaker and his audience.

"At the Moscow Conference," he began, "I was
in an official capacity and my scope was limited, but
here I am Tavarish—comrade. There are people
here who connect me with that terrible affair . . ."
(referring to the Korniloff counter-revolution).

He was interrupted by shouts of "Yes, there are
people here who do!"

Kerensky stepped back as if struck, and all the
enthusiasm went out of his face. One was shocked
by the extreme sensitiveness of the man after so
many years of revolutionary struggle. Deeply con-

scious of the coldness, the hostility even of his audience, he played on it skilfully—with oratory, with pleading, with a strange unabated inward energy. His face and his voice and his words became tragic and desolate, changed slowly and became fire-lit, radiating, triumphant; before the magnificent range of his emotion all opposition was at last swept away. . . .

"After all, it doesn't matter what you think about *me*—all that matters is the revolution. We are here for other business than to heap personal recriminations upon one another!"

Yes, that was true and everybody in the audience felt it for the time he was speaking. When he finished they rose in a tremendous ovation.

Dramatically he stepped from the stage, traversed the long aisle in the centre of the theatre, mounted the Tsar's own box and raising his right hand as if to drink a toast, spoke again: "Long live the Democratic Republic and the Revolutionary Army!" And the crowd shouted back: "Long live Kerensky!"

This was the last ovation Kerensky ever got. If the Russians had the temperament of the Italians or of the French, I think they would have worshipped Kerensky; but Russians are never convinced by phrases and they are not hero worshippers. They were disappointed in Kerensky's speech. He was charming, but he had not told them anything. There were many details about the Korniloff affair which they wished straightened up in their minds, they also wanted desperately to know what had been done about a conference of the Allies to discuss war aims, and he had not mentioned it. An hour after his departure his influence was gone, and they threw themselves into the struggle of deciding the issues for which they had come.

For nine days the Democratic Congress continued. Hundreds of delegates spoke in that time. They had much to say, for how long they had endured silence! At first, the Chairman tried to limit their speeches, but the audience raised a loud clamour: "Let them say everything they have come here to say!"

It was amazing how they could do it. I recall the words of their countryman, Tshaadaev: "Great things have always come from the wilderness." Often a peasant, who had never made a speech in his life, would give a long sustained talk of an hour's duration and keep the close attention of his audience. Not one speaker had stage fright. Few used notes and every man was a poet. They said the most beautiful and simple things; they knew in their innermost hearts what they wanted and how they wanted it. The gigantic problem was to weave a general satisfactory programme from their widely divergent desires. Whenever the chairman announced recess, we would all rush out into the corridors and eat sandwiches and drink tea. The sessions often lasted until 4 in the morning, but the hunger for truth and the liquefaction of difficulties never lessened. There was the same earnest groping for solutions in the grey dawn as in the flaring sunset. . . .

Some events and some personalities stand out sharply from that long fortnight of oratory, when the representatives of over fifty races and 180 million of people spoke all that was in their hearts. I remember a tall, handsome Cossack, who stood before the assembly and, blushing with shame, cried out: "The Cossacks are tired of being *policemen!* Why must we forever settle the quarrels of others?"

I remember the dark, striking Georgian who rebuked the speaker who preceded him because he desired national independence from Russia for his small nationality. "We seek no separate independence," he said, "when Russia is free, Georgia will also be free!"

There was a gentle-looking peasant-soldier who gave solemn warning: "Mark this down well, the peasants will never lay down their arms until they receive their land!"

And the nurse who came to describe conditions at the front, how she broke down and could only sob: "Oh, my poor soldiers!"

There was a stern little delegate who arose and said: "I am from Lettgallia . . ." and who was interrupted by serious interrogations of "Where is that?" and "Is that in Russia?"

They had a slow, ridiculous way of counting votes; it wasted hours. I spoke to one of my neighbours about it, saying we had quite simple methods of doing these things in America. "Oh, time is roubles here," he said, referring to the low exchange, and the correspondents roared with laughter.

As the Congress progressed one had time to note some of the visitors. Mrs. Kerensky was one. She sat in the first gallery, dressed always in black, pale and wistful. Only once did she make audible comment. It was when a Bolshevik was severely criticising the Provisional Government. Almost involuntarily she exclaimed: *"Da volna!—enough!"*

In one of the boxes sat Madame Lebedev, Prince Kropotkin's daughter. She had been so long a part of London society that she appears more English than Russian. She frankly protested against all radical measures and she possessed the only lorgnette in the Democratic Congress; it was the subject of much conversation and not a little resentment among the peasant delegates.

There were a number of Americans in the diplomatic box, including members of the Red Cross Mission. Colonel Thompson and Colonel Raymond Robbins were present at nearly every session and took a lively interest. Robbins often came down to the reporters' quarters and discussed the situation with us.

Among the strong personalities of the delegates were the three sick men—Tcheidze, Tseretelli, Martoff, all suffering from, and in dangerous stages of, tuberculosis. Tcheidze is a Georgian, eagle-eyed, past middle age—a remarkable chairman whose ready wit always was able to subdue the sudden uproars that continually threatened the life of the Congress. It was noticeable that on the only night he was too ill to attend the serious split with the Bolsheviki occurred. Tcheidze is a Menshevik and was at one time a University professor.

Tseretelli is also a Georgian and a Menshevik, and next to Kerensky, at that time, was undoubtedly the most powerful man in Russia. Tseretelli's manner and his whole appearance are so Asiatic that he looks almost absurd in a trim, business suit; it is impossible not to picture him in long flowing robes. He was a member of the Third Duma and his health was broken by seven years of hard labour in Siberia.

Martoff is grey and worn, his voice always husky from throat trouble. He is much beloved by his constituents and is known everywhere as a brilliant writer. Exiled in France for many years, he became one of the principal figures in the labour movement there. He is a Menshevik Internationalist by politics.

Flashing out of that remarkable gathering was

the striking personality of Leon Trotsky, like a
Marat; vehement, serpent-like, he swayed the assembly as a strong wind stirs the long grass. No
other man creates such an uproar, such hatred at
the slightest utterance, uses such stinging words and
yet underneath it all carries such a cool head. In
striking contrast was another Bolshevik leader,
Kameneff, who reminded me of Lincoln Steffens.
His way of expressing his opinions was as mild as
Trotsky's was violent, sharp and inflammatory.

There was the young War Minister, Verkovsky,
known as the only man in Russia who ever was on
time at an appointment. He is one of the most
honest and sincere persons I ever met. It was he
who first had the idea of democratising the army;
it was he who insisted that the Allies be informed of
the alarming morale of the Russian army; he was
a better fighter than a talker. For his frankness
he was dismissed from office by the Provisional
Government.

Not by any means to be overlooked were the
twenty-three regularly elected women-delegates,
notable among them Marie Spirodonova, the most
politically powerful woman in Russia or in the
world, and the only woman the soldiers and peasants are sentimental about.

The one thing that the Congress completely
agreed upon and instructed the Preparliament
which was to follow it to do, was to issue an appeal
to the peoples of the world reaffirming the Soviets'

formula of last spring for peace "without annexations and indemnities" on the basis of self determination of peoples.

A particularly noticeable sore point in all the
speeches was the subject of capital punishment in
the army; it was always causing an unpleasant stir.
The sentiment of the gathering was firmly against
the re-establishment, but it was never actually put
to a vote.

The quarrel over coalition wrecked the assembly and almost broke Russia.

A resolution put up by Trotsky and reading:
*We are in favour of coalition of all democratic
elements—except the Cadets* carried overwhelm-
ingly and showed the real feeling of the country.
Every one knows now that it was the most tragic
thing in the world that that decision was not left.

Unfortunately just after the resolution was
passed word was brought that Kerensky was about
to announce his new cabinet containing representatives of the Cadet party and several Moscow business men known to be particularly out of harmony
with socialistic aims. Tseretelli hurried to the Winter Palace and told Kerensky that he dare not ignore the will of the Congress; that without the sanc-
tion of the Democratic Congress, the formation of
such a cabinet would lead directly to civil war.

The next morning Kerensky appeared before the
Presidium, and threatening to resign, painted such
a tragic picture of the condition of the country, that

the Presidium returned to the Congress with a resolution to immediately constitute the Preparliament with full power to authorise the constitution of a coalition government, if it thought absolutely necessary, and to admit into its own ranks representatives of the bourgeoisie proportional to their representatives in the cabinet.

Tseretelli, Dan, Lieber, Gotz and other politicians upholding the Provisional Government, spoke again and again for the measure. Lunarcharsky and Kameneff spoke against the wording, claiming that Tseretelli had not read the same motion which had been agreed upon at the meeting of the Presidium. Whereupon Tseretelli's usual self-control deserted him and he cried: "The next time I deal with Bolsheviki I will insist on having a notary and two secretaries!"

The Bolshevik Nagine shouted back that he would give Tseretelli five minutes to retract his words, and Tseretelli remaining stubbornly silent, the Bolsheviki used this as an excuse for bolting the assembly. They left the hall amid the most tremendous uproar. Men ran into the hallways, screaming, pleading, weeping. . . .

This split over coalition marked the beginning and the end of many things, and was a real blow to the democratic forces brought together for self-protection during the Korniloff attempt. When the measure was finally voted on the delegates were not allowed a secret ballot and those who voted for

coalition sacrificed their political careers. Just over
night a terrific change came over that once peaceful
gathering. When Spirodonova got up and told her
peasants that this measure cheated them out of their
land, a sullen, ominous roar followed her words.
As I watched that change it came to me what the
passage of the measure really meant. It meant
civil war, it meant a great swinging of the masses
to the banners of the Bolsheviki, it meant new
leaders pushed to the surface who would do the
bidding of the people and old leaders hurled into
oblivion, it meant the beginning of class struggle
and the end of political revolution. . . .

The next evening coalition passed by a small
majority and the delegates filed out into the rain
singing, after having arraigned the elections of the
Preparliament.

CHAPTER VII

THE PREPARLIAMENT AND THE SOVIET OF THE RUSSIAN REPUBLIC

THE first meeting of the Preparliament took place in the shabby old hall of the Petrograd City Duma on September 23, and showed that the moderate socialist machine was still in control by the election of Tcheidze as President. Another indication of the drift toward the right wing was the decision to discuss the question of the constitution of the government in *secret session,* in face of the combined protest of the Bolsheviki, Menshevik Internationalists and the left wing of the Socialist Revolutionists.

During the secret session Tseretelli arrived from the Winter Palace with a report of the alliance, hastily concluded, between the moderate socialists and the bourgeoisie, announcing the bourgeoisie would enter the Preparliament in the proportion of 100 members to each 120 democratic members; that a coalition government would be formed; and that the government would not be responsible to the Preparliament. Then, coalition being a fact, everybody entered into violent debates upon the subject, which were terminated by "Babushka"—Katherine

Breshkovsky—announcing in a trembling voice at
2 o'clock in the morning that coalition was right because human life itself is based on the principle of
coalition. . . .

The next day a heated debate took place upon
the question of the death penalty in the army, followed by passionate addresses by every one altogether upon coalition, the dissolution of the Duma,
peace, the threatening railroad strike and the land
question which ended in the resolution of the Socialist Revolutionists insisting that the first task of the
new government should be the immediate placing
of the land under the authority of the General
Peasant Land Committees.

At one time such pandemonium reigned that a
violent discussion between Trotsky and Tcheidze
ended because neither one could hear what the other
was saying. In the lull that followed Babushka rebuked the delegates, saying that they had come together to save Russia and that not a single step had
been taken.

Avksentieff, at that time president of the Peasants' Soviets, but now completely out of power, declared that if the land amendment had anything to
do with endangering coalition the Socialist Revolutionists would retire it. The whole matter was
finally disposed of by the representative of the
Land Committee himself who got up and remarked
bitterly that the whole business was utter absurd-
ity and that the Peasants' Land Committee would

have nothing to do with it, whereupon the resolution was rejected. At six o'clock in the morning the delegates went wearily home. . . .

The next morning Tseretelli announced that the official name of the *Preparliament* would be the *"Council of the Russian Republic,"* and that it would meet in the Marinsky Palace after a few days.

Thus ended the first attempt to establish absolute democratic power in Russia.

The Council of the Russian Republic

Ever since the split of the democratic forces over coalition with the bourgeoisie, which first definitely manifested itself at the Democratic Congress, a new revolution, deeper and in every way more significant than the first, hung like a thundercloud over Russia.

For weeks the Council of the Russian Republic held futile sessions. On the very first evening the Bolsheviki, through their spokesman, Trotsky, hurled a bomb into the gathering from which it never recovered. They accused the *sens* element—propertied classes—of being represented out of proportion to their numbers as shown from the elections held all over the country, and charged them with the deliberate intention of ruining the Revolution; appealing to the soldiers, workers, peasants of all

Russia to be on their guard, the Bolsheviki left the Council never to return.

After that the Council sat day after day a hostile, divided house, unable to carry out a single measure. The Mensheviki, Menshevik Internationalists, Right and Left Socialist Revolutionists, sat on one side, the Cadets on the other, and the vote on every important measure was a tie. Orators from the right got up and heaped recriminations on the left, orators from the left screamed curses on the right. And all this time the mass of the people left their old parties and joined the ranks of the Bolsheviki. Louder grew the cry: *All power to the Soviets!*

Every few days Kerensky would appear and make impassioned addresses without any effect whatever. He would be received coldly and listened to with indifference; the Cadets often choosing this particular time to read their papers. During one of the last speeches he made in the Marinsky Palace, begging them to forget their differences and somehow pull together until the Constituent Assembly, he was so overcome with the hopelessness of the situation that he rushed from the platform, and having gained his seat, wept openly before the whole assembly.

All those who understood the condition of Russia at that time knew that Kerensky was the symbol of a fictitious union of parties, but how long he could remain so no one could foretell. He was ill and carrying the weight of all Russia on his frail shoulders. Moreover, he had been betrayed by the very Cadets he had worked so hard to keep in the government. The Bolsheviki were offering a definite programme containing the wishes nearest to the hearts of the people, and the people were going over to the Bolsheviki.

One thing might have saved that pitiful Preparliament even in the last days, and that was the *Allied Conference to Discuss War Aims* which new Russia had demanded at the beginning of the revolution and which was to be held in June, was postponed to September, then to November, and finally, apparently, given up altogether. With the final decision of the Allies and the now famous speech of Bonar Law, the last shred of influence of the Council of the Russian Republic disappeared. All Russia was slowly starving, another terrible winter was coming on, and there was nothing definite to hang their hopes on. Kerensky himself was not unaware of the danger or of the confusion. He told me himself a few days before the Provisional Government fell, that the people had lost confidence and were too economically tired to put up further effective resistance against the Germans.

"The Constituent Assembly must be the deciding factor, one way or the other," he said. He hoped that he could hold the country together until then, but I do not think for a moment that he thought he could hold it any longer. I do not think he dared prophesy what would come out of the Constituent when it did meet.

On the 25th of October the meeting of the All-Russian Soviets was due to be held in Petrograd. That that tremendously powerful body would demand immediate action on all the burning issues there was no doubt and that if the Provisional Government refused those demands they would take over the power there was also no doubt. Kerensky believed that he ought to prevent this meeting by any means possible, even by force of arms. He did not realise how far the Bolshevik influence had spread. The masses moved fast in those days and the army had gone solidly Bolshevik.

Kerensky took into account, however, that the Petrograd garrison was composed largely of Bolsheviki and so on the 14th of October he ordered this garrison to the front to be replaced by troops less Bolshevik. Naturally, the Petrograd garrison protested and appealed to the Petrograd Soviet. The Petrograd Soviet appointed a commission to go to the front and confer with General Tcherimissov, and demand of him that if he did send regiments to replace the Petrograd garrison the Petrograd Soviet should be allowed to choose them. This General Tcherimissov flatly refused, saying that he was the Commander-in-Chief of the army and that his orders should be obeyed.

In the meantime members of the Petrograd garrison held a meeting and elected the now famous

Military Revolutionary Committee, and demanded that a representative of the committee be allowed in the General Staff of the Petrograd District. This proposition the Petrograd Staff refused to consider. In reply the Petrograd garrison declared that it would take no orders from anybody unless countersigned by the Military Revolutionary Committee, as they maintained that the General Staff was secretly taking measures to violently disperse the meeting of the All-Russian Soviets.

On the 23rd of October Kerensky announced before the Council of the Republic that an order had been issued for the arrest of the Military Revolutionary Committee. The next night several of the members of the Pavlovsk regiment secreted themselves in the office of the General Staff and discovered that plans were being made to seize the city with the aid of the Junker regiments, and forcibly prevent the meeting of the All-Russian Soviets scheduled for the following day. That night Kerensky ordered all the extreme radical papers and the extreme conservative papers suppressed. But it was too late; it was like sweeping back the sea with a broom. The Soviets had become the ultimate political expression of the popular will, and the Bolsheviki were the champions of the Soviets.

After the Pavlovsk regiment discovered the plans of the Provisional Government, they set sentries and began to arrest all persons entering or leaving the General Staff. Before this time the Junkers

had begun to seize automobiles and take them to the
Winter Palace. They also seized the editorial offices and the printing shops of the Bolshevik papers.
During all this confusion a meeting of the old
Executive Committee of the Soviets was taking
place at Smolny. The old Central Executive Committee was composed largely of Mensheviki and
Left Socialist Revolutionists, and the new delegates were almost solidly Bolshevik. There was
nothing to do but speedily elect a new Central Executive Committee.

The next afternoon I started out as usual to
attend the regular session of the Council of the Russian Republic. One glance around the square before the Marinsky Palace assured me that the long
looked for storm of civil war had come. Soldiers
and sailors were guarding the little bridges over the
Moika, a great crowd of sailors were at the door
of the palace and barricades were being hastily
constructed. Word flew round that they were ar-
resting the Council of the Republic. As a matter
of fact no one thought the Council of the Republic
was important enough to arrest. What really happened was tragically funny. A big Cronstadt sailor
marched into the great elaborate red and gold assembly chamber and announced in a loud voice:
"No more Council! Go along home!" And the
Council went—disappearing forever as an influence
in the political life of Russia.

CHAPTER VIII

THE FALL OF THE WINTER PALACE

OCTOBER 24th was crowded with events. After the ludicrous disbanding of the Council of the Russian Republic at 2 o'clock in the afternoon by the Cronstadt sailors, with two other Americans, John Reed and Albert Rhys Williams, I started for the Winter Palace to find out what was happening to Kerensky.

Junker guards were everywhere. They let us pass after solemnly examining our American passports. Once past the guards we were at liberty to roam all over the palace and so we went directly to Kerensky's office. In the ante-room we found one of his smart-looking aides who greeted us in an agitated manner. Babushka, he told us, had gone two days before and Kerensky had also fled after an embarrassing experience which might have caused his capture. At the last moment he found that he did not have enough gasoline for his automobile, and couriers had to be sent into the Bolshevik lines. . . .

Everybody in the palace was tremendously excited; they were expecting an attack at any minute and no one knew just what to do. There was

79

very little ammunition and it was only a matter of hours before they would have to give up. The Winter Palace was cut off from all outside help and the ministers of the Provisional Government were inside. . . .

When we left Kerensky's office we walked straight to the front of the palace. Here were hundreds of Junkers all armed and ready. Straw beds were on the floor and a few were sleeping, huddled up on their blankets. They were all young and friendly and said they had no objection to our being in the battle; in fact, the idea rather amused them.

For three hours we were there. I shall never forget those poor, uncomfortable, unhappy boys. They had been reared and trained in officers' schools, and now they found themselves without a court, without a Tsar, without all the traditions they believed in. The Miliukov government was bad enough, the Provisional government was worse and now this terrible proletarian dictatorship. . . . It was too much; they couldn't stand it.

A little group of us sat down on a window ledge. One of them said he wanted to go to France "where people lived decently." Another enquired the best method to get into the American army. One of them was not over eighteen. He told me that in case they were not able to hold the palace, he was "keeping one bullet for himself." All the others declared that they were doing the same.

Some one suggested that we exchange keepsakes. We brought out our little stores. I recall a silver Caucasian dagger, a short sword presented by the Tsar and a ring with this inscription: "God, King and Lady." When conversation lagged they took us away to show us the "Gold Room" of which they were very proud. They said that it was one of the finest rooms in all Europe. All the talk was sprinkled with French phrases just to prove they were really cultured. Russia had moved several centuries beyond these precious young men. . . .

Once while we were quietly chatting, a shot rang out and in a moment there was the wildest confusion; Junkers hurried in every direction. Through the front windows we could see people running and falling flat on their faces. We waited for five minutes, but no troops appeared and no further firing occurred. While the Junkers were still standing with their guns in their hands, a solitary figure emerged, a little man, dressed in ordinary citizen's clothes, carrying a huge camera. He proceeded across the Square until he reached the point where he would be a good target for both sides and there, with great deliberation, he began to adjust his tripod and take pictures of the women soldiers who were busy turning the winter supply of wood for the Palace into a flimsy barricade before the main entrance. There were about two hundred of them and about fifteen hundred Junkers

in the whole place.   There was absolutely no food
and a very small supply of ammunition.

At five-thirty we decided to go to Smolny to
be present at the opening of the much-talked-of
meeting of the All-Russian Soviets.

As we crossed under the Red Arch we met a
group of Bolshevik soldiers who were discussing
the best means of taking the Palace.   "The bad
part is," said one, "that the Women's Battalion is
on guard there and they will say we shot Russian
women. . . ."

At Smolny a hot battle of words was being
waged between the Mensheviki and Socialist Revolutionists on one side and the Left Socialist Revolutionists, Bolsheviki and Menshevik Internationalists on the other.   The former were claiming that all important matters must be put off until
after the Constituent Assembly.   But the majority
of the gathering would not listen to them.   Finally,
an inspired speaker declared that the cruiser
Aurora was at that very moment shelling the Winter Palace, and if the whole uprising was not
stopped at once, the delegates from the Menshevik
and Socialist Revolutionist Parties, together with
certain members of the City Duma, would march
unarmed through the firing lines and die with the
Provisional Government.

This came as a complete surprise to many of the
delegates who were to be sacrificed, but nevertheless a number of them impulsively followed the

speaker; others sat uneasily in their seats looking
as if they felt this was carrying party principles
altogether too far.   The affair, dramatic as it was,
did not have much effect on the general assembly;
five minutes after the delegates left the hall they
proceeded with their regular business.   The soldiers
seemed to think it was a particularly good joke
and kept slapping each other on the back and
guffawing.

Of course we followed the bolting delegates.

All the street cars had stopped and it was two
miles to the Winter Palace.   A huge motor truck
was just leaving Smolny.   We hailed it and
climbed on board.   We found we had for compan-
ions several sailors and soldiers and a man from
the Wild Division, wearing his picturesque, long
black cape.   They warned us gaily that we'd probably all get killed, and they told me to take off a
yellow hatband, as there might be sniping.

Their mission was to distribute leaflets all over
town, and especially along the Nevsky Prospect.
The leaflets were piled high over the floor of the
truck together with guns and ammunition.   As we
rattled along through the wide, dim-lit streets, they
scattered the leaflets to eager crowds.   People
scrambled over the cobbles fighting for copies.   We
could only make out the headlines in the half-light:

*"Citizens!   The Provisional Government is
deposed.   State Power has passed into the or-*

*gan of the Petrograd Soviet of Workers' and
Soldiers' Deputies."*

Before I left Smolny I had secured a pass from
the new famous Military Revolutionary Committee. My pass read:

"No. 1
"Military Revolutionary Committee of the
Petrograd Council of Workers' and Soldiers'
Deputies gives Tavarishe Louise Bryant free
passage through the city.
"Signed by the Chairman and Secretary
of the Military Revolutionary Com-
mittee, and stamped by the Military
Division."

Where the Ekaterina Canal crosses the Nevsky,
guards informed the driver that we could go no
further. So we jumped down and found ourselves
witnesses to as fantastic a political performance as
ever took place in history.

Huddled together in the middle of the Nevsky
were the delegates of the Socialist Revolutionist
and Menshevik Parties. Unto themselves they
had since gathered various wives and friends and
those members of the city Duma who were not
Bolsheviki, Left Socialist Revolutionists or Menshevik Internationalists—so that their number was

something over two hundred. It was then two
o'clock in the morning. . . .

For a time, I confess, we were all pretty much
impressed by these would-be martyrs; any body
of unarmed people protesting against armed force
is bound to be impressive. In a little while, however, we couldn't help wondering why they didn't
go ahead and die as long as they had made up their
minds to it; and especially since the Winter Palace and the Provisional Government might be captured at any moment.

When we began to talk to the martyrs we were
surprised to find that they were very particular
about the manner in which they were to die—and
not only that but they were trying to persuade
the sailor guards that they had been given permission to pass by the Military Revolutionary
Committee. If our respect for their bravery weak-
ened, our interest in the uniqueness of their political tricks grew a good deal; it was clear that the
last thing the delegates wanted to do was to die,
although they kept shouting that they did at the
top of their voices. "Let us pass! Let us sacri-
fice ourselves!" they cried like bad children.

Only twenty husky sailors barred the way. And
to all arguments they continued stubborn and un-
moved. "Go home and take poison," they advised
the clamouring statesmen, "but don't expect to die
here. We have orders not to allow it."

"What will you do if we suddenly push forward?" asked one of the delegates.

"We may give you a good spanking," answered the sailors, "but we will not kill one of you—not by a damn sight!"

This seemed to settle the business. Prokopovitch, Minister of Supplies, walked to the head of the company and announced in a trembling voice: "Comrades: Let us return, let us refuse to be killed by *switchmen!*" Just exactly what he meant by that was too much for my simple American brain, but the martyrs seemed to understand perfectly, for off they marched in the direction from which they had come and took up headquarters in the city Duma.

When we showed our passes, it was like magic, the sailors smiled and let us go forward without a word. At the Red Arch, soldiers informed us that the Winter Palace had just surrendered. We ran across the Square after the Bolshevik troops, a few bullets whistled by, but it was impossible to tell from which direction they came. Every window was lit up as if for a fête and we could see people moving about inside. Only a small entrance was open and we poured through the narrow door.

Inside the Junkers were being disarmed and given their liberty. They had to file past the door through which we had come. When those we had been with in the afternoon recognised us they waved friendly greetings. They looked relieved that it was all over, they had forgotten about the "one bullet" they were keeping for themselves. . . .

The Ministers of the Provisional Government were betrayed by the employees in the palace, and they were quickly hauled out of all sorts of secret back rooms and passages. They were sent to Peter and Paul fortress. We sat on a long bench by the door and watched them going out. Tereschenko impressed me more than the others. He looked so ridiculous and out of place; he was so well groomed and so outraged.

The Woman's Regiment, amounting to about two hundred, were also disarmed and told to go home and put on female attire.

Every one leaving the palace was searched, no matter on what side he was. There were priceless treasures all about and it was a great temptation to pick up souvenirs. I have always been glad that I was present that night because so many stories have come out about the looting. It was so natural that there should have been looting and so commendable that there was none.

A young Bolshevik lieutenant stood by the only unlocked door, and in front of him was a great table. Two soldiers did the searching. The Lieutenant delivered a sort of sermon while this was going on. I wrote down part of his speech:

"Comrades, this is the people's palace. This is our palace. Do not steal from the people. . . . Do not disgrace the people. . . ."

It was amusing to see what those great, simple soldiers had taken—the broken handle of a Chinese sword, a wax candle, a coat-hanger, a blanket, a worn sofa-cushion. . . . They laid them out all together, their faces red with shame. And not one thing was of the least value!

About five o'clock the same morning we left the Winter Palace and called at the City Duma. Here we found the indignant and no longer self-sacrificing politicians furiously forming what they ingeniously chose to call the "Committee for Saving the Country and the Revolution."

Soon after it fell into their hands, the Soviet government turned the Winter Palace into a People's Museum.

CHAPTER IX

THE CONSTITUENT ASSEMBLY

I BELIEVE we are more confused over the
Constituent Assembly than over most things
that have happened in Russia. And there is good
reason for that confusion. Following the political developments as closely as I did in those days,
I found it difficult enough to understand. Here
were the radical parties for months shouting for
the Constituent—in fact, ever since the first revolution. At last it was called, suddenly dissolved,
and not a ripple in the country!

Of course the outstanding reason was that the
Constituent voted *against* the Soviets. And that
was a pretty fair test of the Soviets. If any power
in Russia could have broken the Soviets it would
have been the Constituent and the Constituent vanished at the first attempt.

How did it happen? asked a surprised world.
By bayonets? Yes and no. It happened because
the people were with the Soviets and the bayonets
were in the hands of the people; there was no force
to oppose the Soviets.

The Constituent Assembly delegates were elected

on lists made up in September and the Constituent
Assembly was not called until the following January. The elections were held in November. The
method of Russian elections is this: to vote for
party and programme, the candidates being nominated by the Central Committee of the party.
Now the majority of the Constituent Assembly
delegates were Socialist Revolutionists and before
the elections came the Socialist-Revolutionist party
had split. The majority of the members went with
the party of the *left,* but the Central Executive
Committee was still dominated by the *right.* Therefore, the Delegates to the Constituent Assembly did
not represent the real feeling of the country at that
time. Moreover, the elections were held two weeks
after the Bolshevik insurrection, when the country
had not yet completely moved to the left; Bolshevism had not yet accomplished itself. By January, when the Constituent met, the country had
swung. In other words, elections were held for the
supreme organ of the kind of government which
was out of existence.

Marie Spirodonova, who keeps in closer touch
with the peasants than any one I know in Russia,
told me that many of the peasants did not vote at
all and the delegates did not want to come. The
one thing that was clear in their minds was that
the Soviets of Soldiers' and Workers' Deputies
should still go on, no matter what the Constituent

Assembly did. . . . It took four or five weeks for the wave of Bolshevism to hit some of the various centres, but when it did, this was the result produced. As far as I could gather from every source of information available, the people demanded: *all power to the Soviets*—and this was not qualified by anything.

An All-Russian Peasants' Conference was held in Petrograd shortly after the Bolshevik uprising. The majority of the delegates came right Socialist Revolutionists—in three days they had joined the left wing; had elected Spirodonova president and gone over to the Soviets, marching in a body to Smolny. There were two All-Russian Peasants' assemblies—both did the same thing.

The Bolshevik leaders did not know how much power the Constituent Assembly would have, but as time went on one thing was clear—the Soviets and the Constituent Assembly absolutely cancelled each other. The main difference between the two bodies was that the Constituent Assembly *included the Cadets, which the November revolution had been made to put down.*

I was present at the opening of Constituent; it was a terrific performance from beginning to end. About eight o'clock the delegates assembled and the air fairly crackled with excitement. It had been extremely hard to obtain tickets and the Tauride palace was jammed. I sat directly over the presidium in a little gallery reserved for reporters.

Lindhagen, the Socialist mayor of Stockholm, strolled by and whispered to us: "It is going to be a regular wild west show . . . every one is carrying a gun."

Victor Tchernoff, once so powerful with the peasants but discredited because he stood for coalition at the Democratic Congress, was elected President. Whenever he spoke he was hissed and booed by the left. Tseretelli was the only Constituent Assembly member listened to by both sides with respect. Tseretelli is a great man, the finest of all the moderate socialist party leaders. Why Kerensky and not Tseretelli was made head of the nation under the Provisional Government I could never understand. Tseretelli towers above Kerensky as Lincoln does over Buchanan or Cleveland. But middle parties and their leaders can never stand in time of revolution and Tseretelli went down with all the rest.

In opening the Constituent Assembly, Sverdlov, chairman of the Central Executive Committee of the Soviets—the new parliament—read the following declaration, which the Soviet Government demanded should be adopted by the Constituent as its working basis:

"Declaration of the Rights of the Toiling and Exploited People

I

1. Russia is to be declared a republic of the workers', soldiers' and peasants' Soviets. All power in the cities and in the country belongs to the Soviets.

2. The Russian Soviet Republic is based on the free federation of free peoples, on the federation of national Soviet republics.

II

Assuming as its duty the destruction of all exploitation of the workers, the complete abolition of the class system of society, and the placing of society upon a socialistic basis, and the ultimate bringing about of victory for Socialism in every country, the Constituent Assembly further decides:

1. That the socialization of land be realised, private ownership of land be abolished, all the land be proclaimed common property of the people, and turned over to the toiling masses without compensation on the basis of equal right to the use of land.

All forests, mines and waters, which are of social importance, as well as all living and other forms of property, and all agricultural enterprises, are declared national property.

2. To confirm the decree of the Soviets concerning the inspection of working conditions, the highest department of national economy, which is the first step in achieving the ownership by the Soviets of the factories, mines, railroads and means of production and transportation.

3. To confirm the decree of the Soviets transferring all banks to the ownership of the Soviet Republic, as one of the steps in the freeing of the toiling masses from the yoke of capitalism.

4. To enforce general compulsory labour, in order to destroy the class of parasites, and to reorganise the economic life.

In order to make the power of the toiling masses secure and to prevent the restoration of the rule of the exploiters, the toiling masses will be armed and a Red Guard composed of workers and peasants formed, and the exploiting classes shall be disarmed.

III

1. Declaring its firm determination to make society free from the chaos of capitalism and imperialism, which has drenched the country in blood in this most criminal war of all wars, the Constituent Assembly accepts completely the policy of the Soviets, whose duty it is to publish all secret

treaties, to organise the most extensive fraternisation between the workers and peasants of the warring armies, and by revolutionary methods to bring about a democratic peace among all the belligerent nations without annexations and indemnities, on the basis of the free self-determination of nations —at any price.

2. For this purpose the Constituent Assembly declares its complete separation from the brutal policy of the bourgeoisie, which furthers the well-being of the exploiters in a few selected nations by enslaving hundreds of millions of the toiling peoples of the colonies and the small nations generally.

The Constituent Assembly accepts the policy of the Council of People's Commissars in giving complete independence to Finland, in beginning the withdrawal of troops from Persia, and in declaring for Armenia the right of self-determination.

A blow at international financial capital is the Soviet decree which annuls foreign loans made by the governments of the Tsar, the land-owners and the bourgeoisie. The Soviet government is to continue firmly on this road until the final victory from the yoke of capitalism is won through international workers' revolt.

As the Constituent Assembly was elected on the basis of lists of candidates nominated before the November revolution, when the people as a whole could not yet rise against their exploiters, and did not know how powerful would be the strength of the exploiters in defending their privileges, and had not yet begun to create a socialist society, the Constituent Assembly considers it, even from a formal point of view, unjust to oppose the Soviet power. The Constituent Assembly is of the opinion that at this moment, in the decisive hour of the struggle of the people against their exploiters, the exploiters must not have a seat in any Government organisation or institution. The power completely and without exception belongs to the people and its authorised representatives—the workers', soldiers' and peasants' Soviets.

Supporting the Soviet rule and accepting the orders of the Council of People's Commissars, the Constituent Assembly acknowledges its duty to outline a form for the reorganisation of society.

Striving at the same time to organise a free and voluntary, and thereby also a complete and strong union among the toiling classes of all the Russian nations, the Constituent Assembly limits itself to outlining the basis of the federation of Russian Soviet Republics, leaving to the people, to the workers and soldiers, to decide for themselves, in their own Soviet meetings, if they are willing and on what conditions they prefer. to join the federated government and other federations of Soviet enterprise.

These general principles are to be published without delay, and the official representatives of the

Soviets are required to read them at the opening of the Constituent Assembly."

At two o'clock in the morning of November 19th, the "Declaration of the Rights of the Toiling and Exploited People" was put to a vote, and defeated. The spokesman of the Bolshevik party demanded the floor, and read for his faction the following statement:

"The great majority of the toiling masses of Russia, the workers, peasants and soldiers, have demanded that the Constituent Assembly recognise the results of the great October revolution, the decrees of the Soviets regarding land, peace and inspection of working conditions, and above all that it recognise the Soviet government. Fulfilling this demand of the great majority of the Russian working-class, the All-Russian Central Executive Committee has proposed to the Constituent Assembly that the Assembly acknowledge this demand as binding upon it. In accordance with the demands of the bourgeoisie, however, the majority of the Constituent Assembly has refused to accede to this proposal, thereby throwing the gage of battle to the whole of toiling Russia. The Socialist-Revolutionary right wing, the party of Kerensky, Avksentieff and Tchernoff, has obtained the majority of the Constituent Assembly. This party, which calls itself a *Socialist Revolutionist* party, is directing the fight of the bourgeoisie against the workers' revolution, and is in reality a *bourgeois counter-revolutionary* party. In its present state the Constituent Assembly is a result of the relative party power in force before the great October revolution. The present counter-revolutionary majority of the Constituent Assembly, elected on the basis of obsolete party lists, is trying to resist the movement of the workers and peasants. The day's discussions have clearly shown that the Socialist Revolutionist party of the Right, as in the time of Kerensky, makes concessions to the people, promises them everything, but in reality has decided to fight against the Soviet government, against the socialist measures giving the land and all its appurtenances to the peasants without compensation, nationalising the banks, and cancelling the national debt.

Without wishing for a moment to condone the crimes of the enemies of the people, we announce that we withdraw from the Constituent Assembly, in order to allow the Soviet power finally to decide the question of its relations with the counter-revolutionary section of the Constituent Assembly."

Thereupon the Bolsheviki, Left Socialist Revolutionists and Unified Social Democrat Internationalists left the chamber. The remaining delegates continued to make speeches, but there was no heart in what they said; without the radical elements, the Constituent was dead. At three o'clock they passed the following resolution to be sent broadcast to the whole world:

RUSSIA'S FORM OF GOVERNMENT

In the name of the peoples who compose the Russian State, the All-Russian Constituent Assembly proclaims the Russian state to be the Russian Democratic Federated Republic, uniting indissolubly into one whole the peoples and territories which are sovereign within the limits prescribed by the Federal Constitution.

LAWS REGARDING LAND OWNERSHIP

1. *The right to privately own land within the boundaries of the Russian Republic is hereby abolished forever.*

2. All the land within the boundaries of the Russian Republic, with all mines, forests and waters, is hereby declared the property of the nation.

3. The Republic has the right to control all land, with all the mines, forests, and waters thereof, through the central and local administration, in accordance with the regulation provided by the present law.

4. The autonomous provinces of the Russian Republic have title to land on the basis of the present law and in accordance with the Federal Constitution.

5. The tasks of the central and local govern-

ments as regards the use of lands, mines, forests
and waters are:

    a. The creation of conditions conducive to
the best possible utilisation of the country's
natural resources and the highest possible development of its productive forces.

    b. The fair distribution of all natural
wealth among the people.

6. The rights of individuals and institutions to
land, mines, forests and waters are restricted merely
to utilisation by said individuals and institutions.

7. The use of all mines, forests, land and waters
is free to all citizens of the Russian Republic, re-
gardless of nationality or creed. This includes
all unions of citizens, also governmental and public institutions.

8. The right to use the land is to be acquired
and discontinued on the basis prescribed by this
fundamental law.

9. *All titles to land at present held by the individuals, association and institutions are abolished
in so far as they contradict this law.*

10. All land, mines, forests, waters, at present
owned by and otherwise in the possession of individuals, associations and institutions, *are confiscated
without compensation for the loss incurred.*

DEMOCRATIC PEACE

In the name of the peoples of the Russian Republic, the All-Russian Constituent Assembly ex-

presses the firm will of the people to *immediately discontinue the war* and conclude a just and general peace, appeals to the Allied countries proposing to define jointly the exact terms of the democratic peace acceptable to all the belligerent nations, in order to present these terms, in behalf of the Allies, to the governments fighting against the Russian Republic and her Allies.

The Constituent Assembly firmly believes that the attempts of the peoples of Russia to end the disastrous war will meet with a unanimous response on the part of the peoples and the Governments of the Allied countries, and that by common efforts a speedy peace will be attained, which will safeguard the well being and dignity of all the belligerent countries.

The Constituent Assembly resolves to elect from its midst an authorised delegation which will carry on negotiations with the representatives of the Allied countries and which will present the appeal to jointly formulate terms upon which a speedy termination of the war will be possible, as well as for the purpose of carrying out the decisions of the Constituent Assembly regarding the question of peace negotiations with the countries fighting against us.

This delegation, which is to be under the guidance of the Constituent Assembly, is to immediately start fulfilling the duties imposed upon it.

Expressing, in the names of the peoples of Rus-

sia, its regret that the negotiations with Germany
which were started without preliminary agreement
with the Allied countries, have assumed the character of negotiations for a separate peace, the Constituent Assembly, in the name of the peoples of
the Federated Republic, *while continuing the
armistice, accepts the further carrying on of the
negotiations with the countries warring against us*
in order to work towards a general democratic
peace which shall be in accordance "with the people's will and protect Russia's interests."

And now the wily Russian politicians over here,
in the face of this historic document, tell us that
the Socialist Revolutionists of the *Right* and the
Mensheviki are standing for war! They want us
to put down the Soviets so they can go on fighting.
There is no doubt in the world that Russia *must*
push the Germans over her borders.   But why
should we waste a lot of energy putting down a
popular government to perform that task, when
we can help the government that is in power to
do the same thing? At the Constituent Assembly the
moderate socialist parties stood *for confiscation of
landed property without compensation* and *for immediate peace.*   The Soviets can go no further than
that; and there is no reason to believe that the advo-
cates of the Constituent could have brought in the
Allies while *continuing the armistice begun by the
Bolsheviki,* there is no reason to believe that they

would have made a less disastrous peace with the
Germans; there is even reason to believe that the
peace might have been more terrible than it was,
because the Soviets had on their side whatever force
of arms there was.

If we are out of harmony with the Soviets—we
must necessarily be also out of harmony with the
wishes of the Constituent.   That is why I, for
one, do not see the use of splitting hairs over this
matter of approval.   The principal problem for
America is whether or not she desires friendship
with Russia; and friendship was never improved
by mixing in family quarrels.

An hour after the passing of the above resolution
of the Constituent Assembly—it was then four in
the morning—the Cronstadt sailors who were on
guard began to murmur among themselves.   They
were tired and they wanted to go home.   Finally
one cleared his throat and said: "All the good people have gone, why don't you go?   The guards
want to get some sleep. . . ."   So ended the
Constituent.

To quote an English colleague: "The Assembly
died like the Tsardom, and the coalition before it.
Not any one of the three showed in the manner of
its dying that it retained any right to live."

CHAPTER X

KATHERINE BRESHKOVSKY! What richness of romance that name recalls. What tales of a young enthusiast who dared to express herself under the menacing tyranny of a Russian Tsar. An aristocrat who gave up everything for her people; a Jeanne d'Arc who led the masses to freedom by education instead of bayonets; hunted, imprisoned, tortured, almost half a century exiled in the darkness of Siberia, brought back under the flaming banners of revolution, honoured as no other woman of modern times has been honoured, misunderstanding and misunderstood, deposed again, broken . . . Katherine Breshkovsky's life was one of sorrow, of disappointment, of disillusionment, but it was a full life. And when the quarrels of the hour are swept aside her page in history will be one of honour and she will be known to all posterity by that most beautiful name on the long records of aspiring mankind—known always as "Babushka," the Grandmother of the Revolution.

For many years Katherine Breshkovsky has been well known in America; it was to sympathetic

America that she always came for assistance.
Even in prison she kept in touch with her numerous admirers and champions in this country. I
felt a sort of vague connection with her because
she knew friends of mine at home, so she was
one of the first persons I sought out when I
reached Petrograd. Cheap tales, gathered by unsympathetic persons and scattered broadcast
abroad, told of her triumphant entrance into Petrograd and Moscow, her brilliant installation on the
throne of the Tsar in the Winter Palace, which
was rumoured to be draped all in red, how she sat
there enjoying the drunken revels of the Anarchists
that constantly surrounded her.

I had all this in mind the morning I first went
there. Crossing under the famous Red Arch I
came out upon the beautiful Winter Palace Square,
which is one of the most impressive squares in
the world. The immense red buildings stretch
away endlessly, giving one the idea of deliberate
lavishness on the part of the builder, as if he wanted
to demonstrate to an astonished world that there
was no limit to his magnificence and his power.

I stopped at the main entrance and asked for
Babushka. "Babushka?" repeated the guard.
"Go round to the side gate." At the side gate I
found other guards who directed me through a
little garden and I finally entered the palace by a
sort of back door.

The svetzars here told me to climb the stairs to

the top floor, and Babushka's room was the last door along the corridor. The Tsar's private elevator, which he had built in recent years, did not work any more and the stairway wound round and round the elevator shaft.

I was ushered right into her room, which was very small—about the size of an ordinary hotel bedroom. There was a desk in one corner, a table and a long couch, several chairs and a bed. It was the kind of room you would pay two or three dollars a night for in an American hotel. Babushka came forward and shook hands with me.

"You look like an American," she said. "Now, did you come all the way from America to see what we're doing with our revolution?"

We sat down on the couch and Babushka went on talking about America, of which she seemed particularly fond. She mentioned many well-known writers here, and called them "her children." I said, "How does it seem to be here in the palace?"

"Why," she answered artlessly and without hesitation, "I don't like it at all. There is something about palaces that makes me think of prison. Whenever I go out in the corridor—did you notice the corridor?—I have a feeling that I must be back in prison—it's so gloomy and forbidding and dark. Personally, I'd love to have a little house somewhere, with plants in the window and as much sun coming in as possible. I'd like to rest. . . . But I stay here because 'this man' wants me to." "This man" was Kerensky.

There was a touching friendship between Babushka and Kerensky. In the swift whirl of events the old grandmother was in danger of being forgotten, after people got over celebrating the downfall of the Romanoffs. But Kerensky did not forget. He made her think that she was very necessary to the new government of Russia. He asked her advice on all sorts of things, but whether he ever took it or not is very doubtful. He paid her public homage on many occasions and she loved him like a son.

I saw Babushka a good many times after that and found why she lived in this back room on the top floor of the Winter Palace. First, it was because she chose to live there. They had offered her the choice of the beautiful apartments and she had refused anything but this simple room. She insisted on having her bed and all her belongings crammed into the tiny place, and ate all her meals there. I don't know whether it was her long years in prison that made her assume this peculiar attitude, or if it was just because she was a simple woman and very close to the people. She wrote a little biography of herself on the way back from Siberia in which she said:

"When I think back upon my past life I, first of all, see myself as a tiny five-year-old girl, who was suffering all the time, whose heart was breaking for some one else; now for the driver, then again for the chamber-maid, or the labourer or the oppressed peasant—for at that time there was still serfdom in Russia. The impression of the grief of the people had entered so deeply into my child's soul that it did not leave me during the whole of my life."

Very pathetic, indeed, was her description of what it was like to be free. This feeling she never knew until the news of the revolution was brought to her. "The longer the war lasted," she wrote, "the more terrible were its consequences, the brighter were the basenesses of the Russian Government. The cleaner was the unavoidableness of the democracies of all countries getting conscious, the nearer was also our Revolution.

"I was waiting for the ringing of the bells announcing freedom, and I was wondering why the bells made me wait. And yet, when in November last, bursts of indignation took place, when angry shouts were being transmitted from one group of the population to another, I was standing already with one foot in the Siberian sledge and was sorry that the winter road was fast getting spoiled.

"On the 4th of March a wire reached me in Menusinsk announcing my liberty. The same day I was already on my way to Achinsk, the nearest railway station. From Achinsk began my uninterrupted contact with soldiers, peasants, workmen, railway employees, students and numbers of women —all so dear to me."

Babushka believed that the Constituent Assembly would meet and form a government, and Kerensky ought to be the first President. She intended to tour Russia in a sort of presidential campaign. Of course I wanted to go along. There were always a lot of people around Babushka, so she told me to come down early in the morning and we would have a private talk together.

We walked up and down the corridor. I remember a significant thing that she said to me. "If anything terrible happens to my country it will not be the fault of the working people, but of the reactionaries." She said she was afraid of a serious counter-revolution, but she didn't seem to know how or when it would break.

I told her I had come for two reasons: First, I wanted to tour the country with her, and second, I wanted to meet Kerensky. She stopped short and looked at me.

"You're very naïve," she said.

"So were you," I answered, "when you smuggled bombs across the country." Babushka stopped again and laughed merrily.

"That's right," she admitted. "Well, we'll see what we can do. Now, about the tour. I won't have room in my wagon. Will you get another wagon?"

Then she began to depict the hardships of the

trip which I believed, with some logic, I could stand
as well as Babushka, for she was very frail and
much older than her years. At the end of our
talk she gave me a note and sent a girl down with
me to Kerensky.

Babushka is an old lady and is very forgetful.
Often she did not remember in the afternoon what
she had said in the morning. I once spent a most
amusing day in the Winter Palace, accomplishing
none of the things I set out to accomplish. I had
had an appointment with Babushka at ten o'clock.
At ten she was asleep. At eleven-thirty I went in
and we began to talk. Five minutes later three
French officers came to pay their respects. Babushka said they would stay but a moment. They
stayed two hours. All this time I waited in the
adjoining room with a young Caucasian officer,
three girls, two old women and several miscellaneous officials. We discussed everything from psycho-
analysis to the reason why American writers don't
produce better literature. The Caucasian officer
gave me letters to his people in the South, and
with true Russian hospitality—not knowing anything about me—invited me down there to stay for
an indefinite period.

At three o'clock Babushka appeared and was
amazed to see me. We went back to her room and
had tea and black bread. I am sorry that some
of the people who wrote those extravagant stories
could not have seen her as I saw her then with

her short grey hair and her peasant costume; everything about her so simple and unassuming.

She had a plan for educational work which had the approval of President Wilson, and a large fund donated by American philanthropists, but somehow the soldiers and workers did not understand it— they accused her of using the funds for political purposes that were reactionary and against the Soviets. A sad misunderstanding ensued which probably led to all the rumours about Babushka's imprisonment by the Bolsheviki. Nothing of the kind ever occurred. I do not think any one in Russia ever thought of harming Babushka, although she must have been misled into believing this because for a while after the fall of the Provisional Government she was in hiding. But later she lived quietly in Moscow.

There is nothing strange in the fact that Babushka took no part in the November revolution. History almost invariably proves that those who give wholly of themselves in their youth to some large idea cannot in their old age comprehend the very revolutionary spirit which they themselves began; they are not only unsympathetic to it, but usually they offer real opposition. And thus it was that Babushka, who stood so long for political revolution, balked at the logical next step, which is class struggle. It is a matter of age. If Julia Ward Howe were alive—an old woman of eighty—one could hardly expect her to picket for woman's suffrage in front of the White House, although in her youth she wrote the Battle Hymn of the Republic.

CHAPTER XI

KERENSKY

KERENSKY again in the limelight! Kerensky visiting the world's capitals and hobnobbing with the world's potentates! A new Kerensky, reported to have grown a beard to hide his too apparent youth. Socialist—comrade—Kerensky now out of politics—comes thence on a special mission—to explain the revolution! Ah, well and good—the world is surely in need of explanation. But who in any country, in any language, can explain the enigmatic Kerensky?

I was in Russia when he was at the height of his political career, when he received ovations and lived in the palace of the Romanoffs. It was a meteoric career—from the Korniloff rebellion to the November revolution—just three months, until Kerensky was fleeing in disguise; his only following a few political leaders and a handful of Cossacks who deserted him and tried to turn him over to the Bolsheviki. He could not rally a single regiment of soldiers, a single company of sailors, the workmen he had armed to repel Korniloff were his bitterest enemies, using the very same arms against him. Even the reactionaries were bent

113

on his destruction. His faithful friend, General Krasnov, advised him to give himself up after the Cossacks were defeated at Tsarskoe Selo. He promised, begged a moment in which to "compose himself"; and in that moment he escaped, leaving his embarrassed protectors to explain as best they could. Perhaps no popular hero ever had a more ignominious exit. The revolutionists were surprised and hurt. What could he have been thinking of to start civil war—to march with the Cossacks against the people? Was it not for this very act that he branded Korniloff a traitor? Did he not join hands with the very element he had been fighting all his life?

A week passed. From his place in hiding came a hysterical letter which was published in the *Volia Naroda,* beginning, "It is I, Alexander Kerensky, who speaks!" He asked the people to put down the usurpers; life went on as usual. In the same issue of *Volia Naroda* was an editorial apologising for the letter, saying Kerensky was a sick man, a man who had finished his political career, it was best to be lenient with him; and *Volia Naroda* was Kerensky's official organ!

Half a year—almost eight months, to be exact—and no further word from Kerensky. Now and again one wonders what could have happened to him. One remembers that he has always been ill and thinks perhaps the poor fellow has died. Suddenly startling headlines inform us that he is in

London—in Paris—in Washington! Alexander Feodorovitch Kerensky will not stay put. I have a feeling as I write this that whatever I say will be ancient history in the light of new, violent developments in the career of this remarkable character. Perhaps he will star in the movies, perhaps . . . but no . . . he can never be a drawing-room favourite; he is not as cultured as Lenine or Trotsky; he speaks only Russian and a few words of French, while they speak any number of languages, are well up on the classics and even chatter of music. Trotsky looks like Paderevski and Lenine like Beethoven. What chance has he against them? Still—Kerensky is playful, ministers in the Winter Palace claimed that he kept them awake all hours of the night, singing grand opera airs. . . .

I had a tremendous respect for Kerensky when he was head of the Provisional Government. He tried so passionately to hold Russia together, and what man at this hour could have accomplished that? He was never wholeheartedly supported by any group. He attempted to carry the whole weight of the nation on his frail shoulders, keep up a front against the Germans, keep down the warring political factions at home. Faster and faster grew the whirlwind. Kerensky lost his balance and fell headlong. . . .

Everything in Russia was so different from what I had expected it would be. I had been told that the Russians were all for the war—when I got there I heard nothing but peace and the talk of the soldiers was strange talk for warriors. Conditions at the front were alarming. There was a shortage of ammunition, of food and of clothing. Soldiers stood, knee-deep in mud, muttering. Many had no coats and the rain came down in a cold, miserable drizzle; many had no boots. . . . One regiment had been without food for three days except for some carrots they had dug from a field behind the lines. When an army gets to such a pass anything is possible.

This was in October. And in Petrograd the art treasures were all being removed from the Hermitage, the old tapestries stripped from the walls of the Winter Palace. All night long wagons passed my window laden with priceless old treasures bound for Moscow to be stored in the Kremlin. What could it mean except evacuation? Even machinery was removed from some of the factories. In the Council of the Russian Republic, Trotsky got up and asked why they were getting ready to turn Petrograd over to the Germans. The burden of all the speeches was peace. And through all the confusion moved Kerensky, far from serene, occasionally breaking down, crying out from the tribunal, to indifferent ears: "I am a doomed man. I cannot last much longer!"

It was through Babushka that I met Kerensky. She gave me a note one afternoon and I went to

his office to get an interview. A friendly little
Russian girl, one of the numerous secretaries in
the Winter Palace, said that she would arrange
everything. Kerensky's own secretary, Dr. Sos-
kice, was away for a week. I was relieved, because
he was death on correspondents. My friend disappeared into the inner office and came running back.
"Ah, you are fortunate!" she exclaimed. "He says
to come right in."

We entered the beautiful little private library
of Nicholas II. Kerensky lay on a couch with
his face buried in his arms, as if he had been suddenly taken ill, or was completely exhausted. We
stood there for a minute or two and then went
out. He did not notice us. . . .

I had time to note some of the Tsar's favourite
books as I passed along—various classics and a
whole set of Jack London, in English.

"Something serious must be the matter with
your Minister-President," I remarked. "I heard
him speak at the Council of the Russian Republic
a few days ago and in the middle of his speech he
rushed from the platform and burst into tears."

"I know," she said. "He really is hysterical.
If he does not weep there he weeps here; and he
is so dreadfully alone. I mean, he cannot depend
on anybody."

Then she went on to tell me all the things that
were wrong with Kerensky's health. According
to her, he had serious stomach trouble, a badly

affected lung and kidney trouble. The only way he could keep up was by taking morphine and brandy. That cautious correspondent, Ernest Poole, makes the same statement in his last Russian book. It seemed incredible that this man was holding the reins of great, seething Russia.

"How long can he manage it, I wonder?" was my almost involuntary question.

She answered with that outward resignation so peculiar to Russians. "Well, surely not very long. We are going to wake up here some morning and find that there is no Provisional Government." In two weeks her prediction had been carried out.

A few days after my unsuccessful visit to Kerensky a courier brought me a large important looking envelope containing an official invitation for an interview.

Kerensky did everything in his power to keep up the morale of the army. Every week he used to go to the front, visit the trenches and make speeches; but the disharmony grew. The officers refused to work with the soldiers' committees; deep conflict ensued. Kerensky had nothing definite to offer the soldiers; there were no peace plans; he was standing for coalition and they disapproved; he did not dare give the peasants the land; no one was satisfied.

Every time he came back from one of these trips he was more discouraged. He admitted the situation quite frankly. "The masses of the people are

too economically tired to do much more fighting.
And by that," he added gravely, *"I do not mean
that the revolution has failed or the revolutionary
army has failed."*

One week when he was supposed to be at the
front he went out to Tobolsk to visit the Tsar.
The Tsar surprised him by being extremely cor-
dial. Kerensky said that he treated him like a favourite minister and made him feel quite embarrassed. The Tsarina had been haughty with the
guards and they were offended. Kerensky spoke
to the Tsar about it and he agreed that she ought
to be more gracious. Poor, weak Nicholas, for a
lifetime he had made it a point to agree with the last
visitor. I wonder what final conversation he had
with that Red executioner, if indeed he is really
dead.

The guards were suspicious of one of the Grand
Duchesses. They said that they overheard her
talking about Dan, Lieber and Gotz, three of
Kerensky's political supporters, and they thought
the conversation ought to be investigated, "it
sounded so much like German. . . ."

The common gossip in Petrograd was that
Kerensky was to marry a famous Russian actress.
This rumour both Kerensky and the actress denied, rather superfluously, since both of them were
already married and had begun no divorce pro-
ceedings. Madame Kerensky did not live in the
Winter Palace and was never seen with her hus-

band. She lived quietly in another part of Petrograd with her two children. Whatever their relations were, however, she was essentially loyal to her husband. After the Provisional Government fell, she was arrested for tearing off Bolshevik posters from the walls—tearing them off with her bare hands. The soldier who took her to prison found out who she was as soon as the officials began to question her, and he was filled with remorse. He said that he could understand her actions under the circumstances, and begged the officials to let her off. This request was immediately granted.

Kerensky was not blind to the approaching class struggle, but he did not know how to time its appearance. During the last interview he ever gave as Minister-President, he said: "Remember, this is not a political revolution. It is not like the French revolution. *It is an economic revolution,* and there will be necessary in Russia a profound revaluation of classes. And it is a very complicated process for all the different nationalities in Russia. Remember, that the French revolution took five years and that France was inhabited by one people; that France is the size of one of our provincial districts. *No, the Russian revolution is not over—it is just beginning."*

Another statement he made that day, and that I am sure he would still maintain, was in regard to material assistance from America to Russia. I asked him how America could best aid Russia.

"First," he replied, "by trying to understand us—by trying to understand the soul of the Russian people and what they are going through. And secondly," he smiled, "by sending us clothes, machinery and money."

The Associated Press correspondent who was with me at the time asked him if American soldiers would be of assistance. He said that that proposition was not practicable, the difficulties of transportation were too great and besides there were plenty of men in Russia—but no supplies.

Russian politicians here claim that Kerensky is now for intervention by the Japanese, and his secretary in London contradicts all this. In the meantime the masses in his own country, having forcibly ejected him, now go on with their struggles without considering him at all.

CHAPTER XII

Countess Panina

TWO women have been Ministers of Welfare
since the revolution—Countess Panina and
plain citizen Alexandra Kollontay.

Both women I know well and respect for widely
different reasons. Countess Panina was in Peter
and Paul Fortress when I first saw her. She had
refused to hand over ninety thousand rubles in
State funds that was in her possession when the
Bolsheviki came into power. Her trial was one
of the most sensational ever held before a revolutionary tribunal.

A young Russian girl and an active worker in
the Menshevik party, who sat next to me during
Panina's trial, made an interesting comment.

"Yes," she said, "Panina really does like poor
people—she thinks they are *almost* as good as other
people."

This is fundamentally the difference between
Panina and Kollontay, and the reason why one is
much loved and the other has been swept aside in
the public regard after the harsh test of revolution.

And yet there are fine things about Panina. As a liberal she did much for struggling Russia in the time of the Tsar. Her Norodny Dom— People's House—was the only Norodny Dom in Russia where good concerts were cheap enough for the masses to attend. She was never afraid to undertake new and hard tasks. It was she who introduced popular lectures and adult schools. If all the members of her party (Cadets) had been up to her standard, they would never have fallen into their present disrepute. Lenine in one of his pamphlets calls her "one of the cleverest defenders of the capitalistic system."

In appearance Panina reminds one of Jane Addams. She is middle-aged and wears severe English-looking clothes. But somehow her clothes are not at all consistent with her personality. She is gay and amusing and she loves to tell funny anecdotes about the revolution.

Countess Panina considers Alexandra Kollontay her bitterest political opponent. In July, Kollontay was in Peter and Paul Fortress, and Countess Panina was Minister of Welfare; by October things were reversed.

"I followed her course with great pleasure," said Panina, laughing.

"The Bolsheviki are by no means all proletariat," she once told me. "Now take for example Mme. Sumonsen, who was arrested in July for implication in a Bolshevik plot. She was a rich woman, who was thrilled with the mad adventures proposed by these radicals. While I was in prison I came across the weirdest performances of this creature.

"In my cell I had many books, and when I was given my liberty I began to gather my things together. 'Well, you see,' I said to one of the Bolshevik officers, 'that's what you get for imprisoning the bourgeoisie—we immediately begin to collect property.'

"He was not at all impressed.

" 'Why, when Mme. Sumonsen left,' he said, 'she had to have a whole truck to carry her belongings—and even that was not enough. It was necessary to make a second trip. Besides, you never had a moon.'

" 'A moon?' I asked, puzzled.

" 'Yes,' he explained, 'she fitted her cell up with pink satin and wore pink satin robes and had lace covers on her cot. In one corner she had specially arranged a shaded electric light that looked like a stage moon. In the evening she would lie back among the satin cushions and the soldiers and guards would come in and she would discourse cleverly on literature and art—just like a courtesan in the time of the Louis.' "

Only in Russia could such an extraordinary Arabian Nights' tale be a reality.

I asked Panina if she believed in the self-governing of charitable institutions as introduced by Kollontay. Countess Panina flushed with anger and looked at me quizzically.

"Do you mean," she said, "the self-governing of children under six or people over one hundred?"

Then she began to rage against Kollontay.

"I, myself, am frantically democratic!" she exclaimed. "But being democratic and being practical are two different things. All the reforms Madame Kollontay will make now will be at the expense of Russia's unfortunates. The people will pay for these experiments with their lives."

I wanted to remind her that this was true also in her time and in any age, but she was unreasonable on every subject that had to do with Kollontay. Once she even said, "I blame her for the massacre of the officers, and not the poor sailors and soldiers," which was surely a ridiculously unjust statement, for Kollontay would be the last person to think of such a thing.

"This absurd Madame Kollontay," she said, "invites the servants to come and sit in armchairs at her meetings. Such things cannot be! What can they know of social reforms or of technical training? It is putting the feet up and the head down, quite mechanically."

"I cannot understand," I said to Countess Panina, "how you can love Russia so much and still take part in this terrible sabotaging. To me the sabotagers are equal to the invading Germans as enemies of the Russian people."

Panina evaded. "Anyway," she purred, "it has been far from successful. There was nothing very spontaneous about it. The very fact that we were ruining the country, and knew it, made us half-hearted. All of us had to halt somewhere, so there was no thoroughness about it. I, for instance, objected to sabotaging in the schools. As you know, the teachers' strike lasted only three days.

"Education has always been my work. To close the schools was punishing the people for wilfulness by administering darkness. I felt that they needed light more than anything else. I found myself going around arguing that the schools were not a point in question. So that when you come right down to it I am not very much of a sabotager."

"On what points do you disagree with the Bolsheviki?" I asked.

"I disagree with them on every point," she cried, "and I think that their leaders are disgusting."

"But you think that they are honest?"

"I know several that are honest," she admitted reluctantly.

"And they treated you well while you were in prison?"

"Yes, they treated me exceptionally well, but the decision of the Revolutionary Tribunal was not the decision of educated persons; it was absurd from a judicial point of view."

"What will your party do to overthrow the present régime?"

"What can we do?" said Countess Panina help-lessly. "At present the Bolsheviki have the army and most of the workers and peasants. We must be silent and wait."

"I shouldn't think you would want to do any-thing if the Soviet Government is really then the expression of the majority of the Russian people."

We were sitting on a couch in Countess Panina's library. She reached over impulsively and took hold of my arm. "Listen," she said, "you are just naturally a Bolshevik. All Americans are! I can never understand why."

Alexandra Kollontay

Kollontay had written many books on mothers and children and on sociology in general before she was appointed Minister of Welfare.

Although Panina has had all the advantages of an aristocratic training with the best schools and teachers, besides having a natural thirst for knowl-edge, Kollontay is the more cultured of the two. Panina owns one of the best libraries in Russia, has been a member of the City Duma of Petro-grad, a nominee for the Constituent Assembly, and for years took part in public life. She speaks six languages.

Kollontay is more or less self-taught, although she has studied much abroad. She speaks thirteen languages fluently. This is really a comment on the comparative value of every phase of thought or accomplishment of these two women. Kollontay is doubly as thorough as Panina. As Ministers of Welfare these two women held one of the highest political positions of any country.

Unlike most intellectuals, Kollontay instead of deserting the revolution when it became an ugly class struggle and every one else was running, chose that particular time to give her most valuable assistance. That is one of the traits I admire most about Kollontay.

Never an extremist, she believed that in a struggle where the masses are fighting for their freedom against the reactionaries she preferred to stay with the people.

She often disagrees with Lenine and Trotsky, but she told me herself that she would never desert the ranks of the proletariat, "if they made every mistake on the calendar."

When I went to Russia, Kollontay was in prison. She had been exiled because of her views against the Tsar's government. She was shut up again for disagreeing with the Provisional Government. She was known to be a Bolshevik and for that "crime" was arrested at the Russian frontier on the outrageous charge of being a German spy. She was let out again because they could not bring her to trial without any evidence whatsoever. She was re-arrested and imprisoned by Kerensky after the July uprising for having openly said that the Soviet government was the only form for Russia, which was the belief of all the Julyists.

Kollontay was seriously ill during her last imprisonment. Two ancient secret service men of the Tsar's régime were set to guard her, by the Kerensky government. She told me herself that for a month she could not even bathe without the solemn scrutiny of these individuals.

Finally she was released just before the Democratic Congress. It would have been embarrassing to have kept her in prison, since she was one of the leading delegates. It was at the democratic congress that I met Kollontay, and as I watched her work in the months that followed I came to admire her more than any other woman in Russia, except Spirodonova.

She is a slim little person, whose age is hard to determine; sometimes she looks twenty and again much, much older. She works untiringly and, through persistence born of flaming intensity, she accomplishes a tremendous amount. She is one of the best women orators I ever heard. She is always asked to interpret the speeches of the foreign delegates that come to Petrograd. Kollontay dresses very well, which is exceedingly unusual in Russia among women interested in revolutionary ideas.

When Kollontay took over her department she found a terrific chaos, and millions of lives depended on her sanity in dealing with the situation and pulling herself out of a carefully planned political intrigue.

Countess Panina, who had been in charge of the department before Kollontay, true to the principles of the bourgeoisie, had persuaded the higher employees to go on strike.

It is amazing how quickly the bourgeoisie of Russia learned from the working class how to sabotage. The employees hid the keys of the safes and secreted the books and resorted to all manner of underhand acts.

Kollontay called them together and quite calmly ordered them to be locked up. As a matter of fact it was only her long practice in self-control that made it possible for Kollontay to appear so calm. She was really deeply disturbed, and told me afterward that she had a terrific struggle with herself before she was able to give the command for the arrests.

"I kept saying to myself: 'Is this you, Alexandra Kollontay, ordering arrests?' Afterwards I used to lie awake nights and wonder how I did it."

Nevertheless the strikers must have been unaware of her struggle, for they returned the keys and the books early the next morning. The entire strike was broken in three days.

Kollontay called another meeting, which even the lowest servants were asked to attend. She was very frank with them at this meeting. Russia, she explained, was bankrupt; there were little funds to carry on charitable work; no one was to receive even a "good" salary; she herself was to get $50 a month, which is the salary of every commissar.

This came as a great blow to the professional social workers, who up to this time had received as much as 25,000 rubles a year. Kollontay shocked them even more by announcing that thereafter all employees should continue to be present at meetings, which would be held frequently, and that the same consideration would be given to suggestions from scrubwomen as from professional philanthropists. Every one was to have an equal chance of promotion.

I used to go up to Kollontay's office on the Kazanskaya and she explained many of her problems to me. She was very much touched by the way some of her lower employees had responded to her appeal in this crisis. It really was astonishing how much many of these simple and uneducated old servants understood about the work. And when they once realised that they were a part of the larger plan they gladly worked for sixteen hours a day to help Kollontay, whom they all called "Little Comrade."

The work of her department covered a vast field, touching all Russia. "One of my greatest tasks," said Kollontay, "is to change the whole system which takes care of the two and a half million maimed soldiers, who are absolutely destitute. If they could feel that they are in some way helping to support themselves, it would add so much to their general happiness. As it is, they don't receive enough money to exist decently; they live in filth and beg for crusts. When I took over the department the highest pension paid to these dependents was thirty rubles a year (about $15 in normal times).

"By cutting down salaries and stopping all kinds of leakage," she continued, "I managed to bring it up to 216 rubles. But even that does not touch what it should be. I believe that the minimum for entirely incapacitated soldiers should be at least 2,400 rubles a year. To do that would require a budget of 4,000,000,000 rubles.

"This two million and a half maimed does not include the sick and wounded, of which there are 7,000,000. And there are 350,000 war orphans in homes alone, and 200,000 deaf, dumb and blind, besides all the insane and the delinquents."

One way by which Kollontay secured money for immediate needs was by placing an exorbitant tax on playing cards, which had to be purchased through her department. Playing cards in Russia, as in most continental countries, have always been a government monopoly, and the profits go to charity. Kollontay increased the price from thirty rubles for a dozen decks to 360 rubles.

One of her dearest ambitions for years has been to establish a home for convalescent mothers known as the Palace of Motherhood. This work is actually being carried out, and what few physicians remain in Petrograd are keenly interested in it.

On Kollontay's suggestion, the Bolshevik Government passed a measure providing free care for sixteen weeks for women before, during and after confinement. When they leave the home they can go back if they are not well, and they are required to work only four hours a day in the factories for the first month after returning. This applies to all women, whether married or single. The Bolsheviki believe that this care of mothers is one of the first debts to the State.

The foundling homes are a terrible problem. Russia has long been famous for the slaughter of her infants, mostly through starvation or neglect. Kollontay arranged a plan whereby children are taken care of by peasant women in their own homes, where they are treated as members of the family.

Every child in Russia now attends public school. All private institutions are officially abolished. Not only the children in prisons, in reform schools and in orphan asylums now must go to public schools, but also the children of the aristocracy must attend these same schools.

"In free Russia," said Kollontay, "there will be neither segregation nor aristocracy in children's education."

One day when I went to see Kollontay a long line of sweet-faced old people were standing outside her door. They had come as a delegation from one of the old people's homes. Kollontay explained their presence.

"I have removed the people who used to be over them and turned their institutions into little republics. They come in every day now and express their gratitude. They elect their own officers and have their own political fights; choose their own menus——"

I interrupted her. "What would that consist of in the present day?" I asked.

Kollontay burst out laughing. "Surely," she said, "you must understand that there is a great deal of moral satisfaction in deciding whether you want thick cabbage soup or thin cabbage soup!"

And this was the whole secret of Kollontay's success, that she allowed other people to make their own decisions.

Kollontay spoke to me about American assistance only two days before I left Russia. She hoped, she said, that trained people interested in her work would come to her aid. There is such a pitiful lack of everything in Russia to-day. Surgical dressings, for example, have to be used over and over again, and good doctors are almost impossible to find.

CHAPTER XIII

LENINE AND TROTSKY

L ENINE and Trotsky! How inflamed we become at the mere mention of those names. After our written sentences, after our thoughts, follow violent vociferations, ejaculations, roars of impatient disapproval; it appears impossible for Anglo-Saxons to judge these men calmly and yet judge them we must and with the finest degree of deliberation. In all fairness to ourselves and the cause of liberty, we must make an unprejudiced decision. They have come to stand for certain ideals of internationalism behind which are certain powerful and growing world forces; we must choose them or men like them, who follow in their footsteps, for friends or enemies. They have become symbols and symbols are as hard to efface as mountains. Symbols cannot be kicked over in sudden anger, passed by with a shrug of the shoulders; symbols decide our destinies . . .

Why do you take off your hat when you stand at the grave of Lincoln? He has become a symbol. Why do you centre your hate on Wilhelm II instead of his millions of subjects? He has become a symbol. President Wilson is a symbol; he has become the interpreter of the Allied war aims. As a personality he is quite detached, but he represents a national ideal. Lenine and Trotsky, especially Lenine, are symbols representing a new order. Lenine stands before us, spokesman of the Soviets, and the Soviets are Russia. We must be intelligent and we must reckon with Lenine. It would be a sad fact to prove that there is no basis for friendship between two great republics. I know there cannot be friendship between the Imperial German Government and the Soviets, but I sincerely believe understanding is possible between the United States and Russia. I give such facts as I have toward that proof:

Friendship must be built on understanding, on frankness. Reports about Russia should not be coloured by imagination, personalities must not enter in. Supposing that we grant that the ideals of the Soviet government are not the ideals of the American democracy. And supposing, after careful consideration, we grant also that the ideals of other nations, entirely friendly toward us, are also not our ideals. Take Japan, for example, or Korea —there is a wedge for common ground. If we could "wash our hands of Russia" as one statesman so *unwisely* said, we would not have to be bothered by weighty considerations; but that is not possible. To do so would be to voluntarily give Germany such added power as to make her invincible; when Germany is able to swallow the Rus-

sian revolution, she will be able to swallow the rest
of the world. And above all, to abandon Russia
or to allow her destruction would place us in the
embarrassing position of abandoning our main reasons for entering the war—"making the world safe
for democracy" and the "self determination of peoples."

It is not easy to write fairly of Lenine, I confess
that. For example, if a reporter were to interview two representative Russians, Lenine and
Kerensky, he might easily throw all the weight of
his argument in favour of Kerensky because he
liked him best. Kerensky has "personality plus,"
as Edna Ferber would say; one cannot help but be
charmed by his wit and his friendliness; he is a
lawyer and a politician. On the other hand, Lenine
is sheer intellect—he is absorbed, cold, unattractive,
impatient at interruption. And yet here are the
facts: Kerensky is spokesman for the defunct Provisional Government; he is discredited; he has no
power in Russia. It would be as silly to try to reestablish him as if some outside force would try to
place William Jennings Bryan in the White House
and eject Wilson. Lenine has tremendous power;
he is backed by the Soviets. Therefore, if the people of Russia have eliminated Kerensky, we must
also eliminate him in our Russian relations. As
long as Lenine is head of the Soviet government
we must assuredly deal with Lenine.

Our most deep-rooted prejudice against Lenine

is that he is accused of being pro-German. I could never find evidence of that; I tried very hard. All I could find out about Lenine forced me to the opposite conclusion; to the conclusion that he plans the destruction of every great German institution, especially Prussian militarism. Lenine's co-workers in Germany are Karl Liebknecht, Rosa Luxemburg, revolutionists and arch enemies of the German government. We, as Americans, are more or less committed to that stand—we have avowed a desire that the present German autocratic government be overthrown. The only element in Germany striving toward that end are the followers of Lenine's philosophy. And if it comes to a choice of accepting as allies one or the other of those two diametrically opposed forces, Prussianism or Socialism, in a fight for world freedom, we cannot hesitate to choose Socialism; and by that I do not mean we have to embrace it. . . .

Lenine is a master propagandist. If any one is capable of manœuvring a revolution in Germany and Austria, it is Lenine. He has lived long in Germany, and he understands German psychology. Gorky has described him as a chemist working with human material instead of chemicals; working just as coldly and as disinterestedly—without regard to human life. So worked all the conquerors, Charlemagne, Napoleon, William Pitt . . . Lenine is monotonous and thorough and he is dogged; he possesses all the qualities of a "chief," including the absolute moral indifference which is so necessary to such a part.

He writes treatises on philosophy and philosophic method; he is an authority on economics; he writes books so scholarly that only sociologists can comprehend them and, at the same time, he appeals to the peasants with pamphlets that are marvels for simplicity.

A hand-bill written by Lenine and signed by both Lenine and Trotsky, was brought to me from the German trenches by a Russian soldier who went over the lines during the armistice. I quote illuminating portions:

"Brothers, German soldiers, follow the example of your great comrade, Karl Liebknecht, leader of international socialism, who in spite of terrific difficulties has carried on a brave struggle against the war—by means of hand-bills and newspapers, numberless strikes and demonstrations. In this fight your government has put thousands of your comrades in jail.

"Finally, there was the heroic stand of the sailors in your fleet, which was very reassuring that fully half the intelligent working people of your country are now prepared for a decisive struggle for peace.

"If you will be helpful to us in our undertaking to establish the union of the workers and peasants and the gradual transition to Socialism in Russia —an undertaking which presents for Russia alone many grave difficulties—then with your capacity for organisation, your experience, your preparation in working class development, we will be infallibly assured of the transition to socialism.

"Hasten to our help in the name of the Workers' and Peasants' Government. . . ."

It would have been impossible for the German officials to have given permission that such propaganda be distributed broadcast under any circumstances. The effects are already too evident.

Louis Edgar Browne, correspondent for the Chicago *Daily News* and the New York *Globe,* recently returned from Russia, makes the following statement:

"Bolshevik culture, through underground methods, is undermining the Austrian Empire. There are 20,000 Bolshevik agitators and revolutionists hard at work in Austria. These agitators are all paid agents of the Soviet government."

And as we are well aware, Austria is cracking open with the fires of revolution.

To-day German papers are forced to admit that German prisoners fighting with the Red Guards, when captured by their countrymen and asked to explain their extraordinary conduct, state that they are internationalists, fighting for the principles of internationalism as opposed to German imperialistic principles.

Trotsky is much more human than Lenine.

Nothing could illustrate this better than their controversy over the signing of the Brest-Litovsk treaty. Lenine wanted to accept the first German peace terms, bad as they were; Trotsky wanted to fight for better ones. Trotsky it was who staged the Brest-Litovsk negotiations and insisted that the negotiations be public. He played for three things: that the Allies join in, that the German revolution commence and that the aims of the Soviets be known throughout the world. Lenine believed that it was absolutely necessary to have a respite, time to firmly establish the Soviet state and to organise an army and propaganda against the German government. Everything turned out as he predicted at Brest. It was all disastrous, yet President Wilson, himself, praised the honesty of Trotsky's stand. Trotsky did not want to sign the treaty and refused to do so. When his hopes of a German revolution were disappointed, his desire was to call all Russia to arms, as the French rose in 1792 to protect their revolution. Trotsky had timed a revolution in Finland, a revolution in the Ukraine and one in Germany and Austria. The last failed to materialise. Lenine, in anger at his failure, called him a "man who blinds himself with revolutionary phrases." Both men now agree that a huge fighting force is necessary for Russia. Lenine's idea is to save as much of Russia as possible by a temporary peace and, in the meantime, to build up the army, systematically, instead of trying to fight trained German soldiers with hastily constructed forces.   To use his own words:

"We are compelled to submit to a distressing peace. It will not stop revolution in Germany. We shall now begin to prepare a revolutionary army, not by phrases and exclamations . . . but by organised work, by the creation of a serious, national, mighty army."

It was the adoption of Lenine's decision by the Soviets that led Trotsky to give up his position as Minister of Foreign Affairs and become Minister of War, bending all his energies towards forming an adequate Red Army.   He has stated that he will accept the services of American officers in training that army; he sees "no reason why Russia and America should not ride in the same car for a way as long as they are following the same road. . . ."

There is evidence that American opinion is slowly swerving also to that view.   The Chicago *Daily News* prints the following editorial, which shows an intelligent and sympathetic understanding of our future relationship to the Soviets and their leaders:

"Most of us in America do not believe in Lenine, most of us do not believe in the Bolsheviki.   Very well.   But it is absolutely necessary for us to believe in the Soviet.   The strength of our belief in the Soviet is the strength of our chances of success in Russia.

"The Soviet is the soul of Russia—and more . . . the Soviet has become its communicating nervous system and its deciding brain.

"Between the Soviets and us there is a bridge— the bridge of common belief in common humanity. Let us cross that bridge now. . . . Beyond it lies the heart of Russia. And through that heart lies the only road to a re-establishment of the Eastern Front.

"Let us abandon every word of unnecessary criticism against Russia. In Russia's house we shall be guests. It is a Soviet house. If the Soviets choose Lenine to rule their house, it is their house. If they choose some one else to rule their house, it is their house.

". . . It is a republic of Soviets, in the mouth of every American the word Soviet must become a word of friendship, a word of comradeship, a word of great hope for a great irresistible alliance against Berlin."

If we are really able to accomplish what the *Daily News* suggests, we will have solved the problem. We will have thwarted the scheme of German agents and ultra-conservatives to create in America an irreconcilable hatred against the Soviets and their representatives.

In appearance, Lenine is very different from the old prison photograph, now used by newspapers, which was taken years ago when he was sentenced to Siberia. He is a little round man, quite bald and smooth-shaven. For days he shuts himself away and it is impossible to interview him. We used to catch him after lectures—then he would chat of inconsequential things.

Lenine comes from an old Russian family and his real name is Ulianov. He is not a Jew. His brother was one of the revolutionary martyrs, and was publicly executed. His father and Kerensky's father were directors in the same school. The execution of Lenine's brother is said to have been one of the greatest influences in Kerensky's life. Neither Lenine nor Trotsky were forced into the revolutionary struggle by circumstances. Their people were not peasants. Trotsky's father was a wealthy Moscow merchant.

Lenine objected to elaborate legal plans for transferring either lands or industries into the hands of the proletariat. He believed that the central authority should have nothing to do with this transference, that it should be accomplished by direct revolutionary action on the part of the local workers and peasants. As early as the end of November all the landlord holdings in Russia had passed into the hands of the peasants and if the Soviet Government had fallen then, still it would have been impossible to return the land to its owners. The same thing was largely true of the factories. This is, of course, the factor which makes it so particularly difficult for the Germans to re-

store capitalism in Russia—without which all attempts of the Germans to exploit Russia are absolutely futile.

During the first days of the Bolshevik revolt I
used to go every morning to Smolny to get the latest news. Trotsky and his pretty little wife, who
hardly ever spoke anything but French, lived in
one room on the top floor. The room was par-
titioned off like a poor artist's attic studio. In one
end were two cots and a cheap little dresser and in
the other a desk and two or three cheap wooden
chairs. There were no pictures, no comfort anywhere. Trotsky occupied this office all the time
he was Minister of Foreign Affairs and many dig-
nitaries found it necessary to call upon him there.

Outside the door two Red Guards kept constant
watch. They looked rather menacing, but were
really friendly. It was always possible to get an
audience with Trotsky.

Running a government was a new task and often
puzzling to the people in Smolny. They had a certain awe of Lenine, so they left him pretty well
alone, while every little difficulty under the sun
was brought to Trotsky. He worked hard and was
often on the verge of a nervous breakdown; he became irritable and flew into rages. For a long time
he refused to use a stenographer and laboriously
wrote out all his letters by hand. A few months
of experience, however, made him change his methods. He got two efficient stenographers and the

Red Guards were replaced by aides who had once been officers in the regular army.

Trotsky is slight of build, wears thick glasses and has dark, stormy eyes. His forehead is high and his hair black and wavy. He is a brilliant and fiery orator. After knowing him the stories about German money seem utterly absurd. He steadfastly refused to take money from his father, in exile he was desperately poor. Both Lenine and Trotsky live with great frugality. Both receive, at their own request, but fifty dollars a month as the highest officials of the Russian government. I think a psychoanalyst would say of Trotsky that he has a "complex" about money. He was so afraid of plots to implicate him that he threw people out of his office when they came to offer honest and legitimate financial aid to Russia.

Lenine and Trotsky are always menaced by assassination. I once was present when three shots were fired at Lenine. He was as cool as if he had been made of stone. In spite of these attempts they go about freely and unprotected. I attach no political importance to these attempts. They are individual acts of violence countenanced by no large group.

The most ludicrous piece of team work ever performed by Lenine and Trotsky was their action in connection with the Roumanian Ambassador. Some Austrians had disarmed a whole division of Bolshevik troops on the Southwest Front (in Roumania) while the fraternising was going on. Trotsky was at Brest and he immediately telegraphed to Petrograd ordering the arrest of the Roumanian Ambassador. No one had ever heard of such a performance, just as they had never heard of publishing secret documents and other unprecedented acts. The next day the entire diplomatic corps in Petrograd went in a body to Smolny. I believe there were thirty-nine. Lenine, when he first beheld them, thought for a joyful moment that all the nations of the world were sending their representatives to recognise the Soviet government.

Lenine was in high good humour; it was not his wish to put out the pleasant gentlemen who called and protested. If it was so unprecedented, if they really did feel so badly because of the imprisonment of their colleague, he assured them politely that he would issue orders for his immediate release. He shook hands with all the thirty-nine and the affair seemed happily ended.

But alas! No sooner had the diplomats rolled home in their comfortable cars and sat down to dinner and began to remark that Lenine and Trotsky were, after all, not such unreasonable fellows than couriers came in with the alarming news that while the Ambassador had indeed been given his freedom, a new order had just been issued calling for the arrest of the Roumanian king! The diplomats sighed hopelessly, for, after all, a king is just a king and entitled to no diplomatic courtesies. . . .

CHAPTER XIV

A TRIUMVIRATE

Antonoff

THE Army and Navy of the Soviet Government, after the November revolution, was directed by a committee of three men—Dubenko, Krylenko and Antonoff. All three had risen from the common soldiery—only one had attended an officers' school. All of them were under thirty, a notable feature of the proletariat revolution so full of youth and of the fiery intensity of youth.

Antonoff, who is at present assisting Trotsky in organising the Red Army, counts for his largest support on the voluntary services of the young men and women of Russia who are surging in like the full tide to save the revolution. As newly appointed Commissar of Petrograd he has charge of the defense against the Germans.

Antonoff looks like a poet. His face is delicate, his hair is long and bushy and he usually wears a bow tie. The bushy hair and the bow tie are by no means a pose. I doubt very much if Antonoff ever thinks about his clothes, or if he cares that his is not the usual costume of a Minister of War. He was a captain in the Russian army before the 1905 revolution. After its dismal failure he had to flee abroad. He has always been an active revolutionist. To military men he is known as an extraordinarily clever strategist.

Some of the most ridiculous things happened to Antonoff just after the Bolsheviki came into power. He had suddenly been elevated to a position of great authority, and everything was in such a chaotic state that he had to go on attending to his customary tasks together with his new duties until other officers could be properly shifted.

One day in November he went to the telephone exchange, which was a point bitterly contested for by both sides. The last he had heard it was safe in the hands of his own men, so naturally, he was surprised to walk in and find himself a captive in the hands of the Junkers. He was entirely unperturbed and sat down in a corner and began to read Dostoievsky . . .

The Junkers had taken the telephone exchange by a very clever ruse. All the uniforms were alike, so it was impossible to tell one side from the other. They found out the hour that the Bolsheviki changed guards, and a few minutes before the time to relieve them the Junkers sent their own men around. No one suspected anything, and Antonoff, playing in exceedingly poor luck, happened to come in almost immediately after the Junker guards had taken charge.

As soon as the Bolsheviki found that the Junkers were in possession of the telephone exchange, they surrounded the building, and for a while a rather fierce battle ensued. But the Junkers soon ran out of ammunition, and reinforcements failed to come, so they had to surrender Antonoff as well as themselves after a few hours.

The next day I went to Smolny with Alexander Gomberg, a Russian from America. Antonoff was in the courtyard preparing to go to Pulkova, just outside Petrograd, where the Red Guards were digging trenches to hold a front against the advancing Cossacks.

We asked Antonoff if we could go along. He assented absent-mindedly, but when we were ready to start we found there was not nearly enough room. Two officers and a courier with a folding bicycle, besides the Minister of War, had to be tucked away in a one-seated car. They consulted a moment and decided that no guests were necessary. Just as the car began to move, Gomberg jumped onto the running board. I didn't have the energy to follow and I have regretted it ever since, because he had an amazing experience. In fact, many of the things that occurred in Russia in those days were so much like Mexico in the time of Villa's triumph around Chihuahua that we found ourselves continually commenting on the fact.

On the outskirts of Petrograd the overloaded automobile broke down. Just what happened to it

I do not know, but it was something very vital, because it had to be abandoned. The Minister of War and the officers and the courier were feeling highly discouraged when along came a large car with a soldier at the wheel. He was returning from the front. Antonoff held him up.

"I'm sorry," he said, "but I will have to requisition your car—mine seems to be finished."

The soldier had no respect for authority. "You can't take my car," he announced with great finality. "I'm going back to get supplies for the First Machine Gun Regiment. They don't need any more men, they need bullets."

Antonoff looked very serious. "But I am the Minister of War," he objected.

The soldier swore joyfully. "Why, you're the very man I need," he exclaimed. "You are to sign the order for more supplies."

Antonoff felt in his pocket for a pencil. He had none. Gomberg supplied an American fountain pen and a notebook. And the order was signed.

"And now," said Antonoff, "how about the machine?"

"Oh, that's settled," called the soldier, pressing the electric button on his self-starter, and off he went in the direction of Smolny.

The next victim was a wealthy speculator. Antonoff extracted his car from him with very little difficulty. Before proceeding, however, he bethought him of the fact that he had taken no food.

There was a little grocery store not far away. Antonoff ordered one of his officers to purchase some dried fish or whatever else he could find. The terrible calamity soon became known that neither the War Minister nor the officers nor the courier had any money. Gomberg made the purchases.

Antonoff is not so irresponsible as this story might make him seem. He had been under a particularly heavy strain and had had no sleep for three nights.

Alexander Gomberg, in spite of these services to the new proletarian government, was abandoned along the muddy front, and after walking a few miles, met a farmer going to Petrograd with a load of hay, who took compassion on him and carried him back to town. He arrived about dawn in a heavy rain, but was quite cheerful.

"It's a funny story," said Gomberg to me, "and if I had ever worked on any part of a paper but the advertising department I would write it up myself."

Krylenko

Krylenko was a student officer before 1905, and was a member of the Social Democratic party. He was in prison many times for his revolutionary activities and at last escaped abroad after the dismal failure to overthrow the Tsar in that year.

When the February revolution broke out he returned to Russia and joined the army. It was largely due to his influence that the Russian army turned Bolshevik. Kerensky feared Krylenko, but did not dare to curb him, knowing how much he was adored by the soldiers.

Krylenko's peculiarly daring personality always won instantly the confidence of his men. He is a good fighter, and has enormous powers of persuasion. And oratory will for a long time play a large part in government in Russia, in spite of Lenine's contempt for the "malady of revolutionary phrases."

I once saw Krylenko do a remarkable thing. It was in the first days of the Bolshevik uprising and certain garrisons had almost been persuaded by the City Duma to remain neutral so that when Kerensky and his Cossacks arrived the Soviet forces would not be well backed up. A great deal depended on the way the *brunoviki* (armoured car division) went. For days Kerensky had sent them out through the city to terrify the opposition. They would come hurtling down a crowded street with their screaming sirens, and the population would run for shelter. On the sides of the cars were still painted in red letters the names given them by the Tsar's government. It was amusing to see the names of all the ancient rulers flash by in a terrible procession. It was as though they had come back from the dead to curse the new order. In spite of the fact that Kerensky ordered the cars out, and they had gone out, no one felt certain that when the fighting began they would be on his side.

One night in early November a meeting was called in the huge Mikhailovsky manège, once the exercising ground for the best-blooded horses in the world, and now used as a barn for armoured cars. The speakers mounted to the top of one of the cars and thousands of soldiers crowded to the very edge of this strange rostrum, listening intently. The great room was blue with cigarette smoke and hazy in the candlelight.

The first two speakers were for Kerensky. They were received for the most part in silence, but as each finished there was applause from the majority. I thought as I watched that Kerensky could count on the *brunoviki,* and in that case he could hold Petrograd. At any rate, it looked as if they would not go against him, perhaps they would remain neutral.

When the first two speakers had ceased, a stocky little man climbed up the sides of the car. He had short legs and a large head and sharp, squinting little eyes. It was Krylenko. For two nights he had not slept, and he had but a few minutes before arrived on a train from the front. His face was so white and he looked so tired that it seemed foolish to bother about him. His cause seemed hopeless.

Then he began to speak.

Krylenko has the ardour of "Billy" Sunday. As

his voice rose over that huddled crowd of soldiers the atmosphere changed rapidly. Men began to move around, to argue with one another; there was no more polite silence, eyes flashed. . . .

He talked about fifteen minutes. When he finished there was no applause, but a great roar, "All Power to the Soviets!" Krylenko stepped back smiling and showed his teeth in a tired grin. The chairman came forward and asked for the vote. There were 3,000 soldiers; all but 25 went with Krylenko. One of the twenty-five said to me: "He's a devil, that man Krylenko!" After the decision was reached Krylenko slid down from the evil-looking machine and disappeared into the night.

Military men have told me that he has unusual ability as an officer; besides he is bent, above all things, on stirring up revolution in Germany and Austria-Hungary. He is a violent little person and reminds one of characters from the most vivid pages of the French revolution. He was always saying publicly and privately: "Those who do not work shall not eat!"

During the negotiations at Brest-Litovsk, Krylenko went along the front and helped get revolutionary literature over the lines. One day the Germans confiscated in their own trenches a hundred thousand copies of "Die Fackel," a paper printed in German by the Russian Foreign Office. There was wild excitement—the German soldiers had already

read the paper and it gave most of them their first
news of what the revolution in Russia aimed to give
to its oppressed people. It told the German soldiers what a revolution in their own country would
do for them. There were, for instance, illustrations of workmen in Petrograd prying off the imperial insignia from buildings, and a picture of the
old German embassy in Petrograd with the query:
"Why don't you send a German workman to represent you to the workmen's and soldiers' government of Russia?" No advance on the French front
would have alarmed the German officers to a
greater degree.

The next day the German delegates at Brest
threatened to break off all negotiations if this propaganda continued. Krylenko, with a smile, ordered that no more literature should be sent. The
soldiers understood the smile and laughed good-
naturedly. "It's beginning to work over there—
like yeast," said one. And the Foreign Office also
understood. They began to work twenty-four
hours a day instead of twelve. Tons of revolutionary pamphlets were smuggled in to the Germans,
and Bolshevik speakers sneaked over No Man's
Land into the enemy's country. At one time forty
of them were in a German insurrection camp and
Krylenko and all the officers knew who they were
and what they were doing.

Dubenko

Dubenko is only 25 years of age. Through his popularity and his marked ability he was elevated in the spring of 1917 from an ordinary seaman to chairman of the Central Executive Committee of the Baltic fleet, and as the whole Russian army and navy is managed by committees, this office is the highest in the fleet.

As the Revolution progressed he became one of the most influential Bolshevik leaders and Cronstadt, which is the home of the Baltic fleet, followed him in his political affiliations and opinions almost en masse. He had a great deal to do with the solid Bolshevik ranks that grew up in the fleet. After the Bolshevik uprising he was virtually head of the navy on the committee with Antonoff and Krylenko. He was active field commander against Kerensky.

Revolutionary discipline amid all the intensity of that tremendous upheaval which will be known to history as the first proletariat revolution was largely due to the Cronstadt sailors. Through all that intensity they moved splendidly with a fervour that created around them forever a legendary glamour—loved and depended upon by the people —feared and hated by the aristocracy and the counter-revolutionists.

They were true moralists, the sailors; for they

cleaned first their own house before they went abroad to sweep up the dirt of others. In Cronstadt they posted notices forbidding all drunkenness, and thieves were punished by death. Their method was picturesque as well as severe. Thieves caught in the act were taken to the edge of a cliff and shot.

Wine produces different effects on different races. On the Russian soldier it does only one thing—it brings out his most bestial tendencies. It was extremely dangerous for the cause of the revolution if the soldiers and sailors or the Red Guards would grow slack in regard to prohibition. There was enough wine in the cellars of the palaces and various warehouses and private houses to keep most of Russia drunk for several years.

Early in January the Cadets hatched a sinister plot. The masses were hungry and cold and in rags. They calculated that it was the psychological moment to open the wine cellars and start a reign of terror, and that by breaking down the revolutionary discipline they could easily take over the power.

I will never forget the night I came up the street and met five roaring, drunken soldiers. They were like animals. I could have sat down in the snow and cried, only I didn't have time. We were near the Winter Palace, and just at that moment a crowd of Cronstadt sailors ran around the corner and, screaming curses on their drunken brothers, they opened fire. One soldier was killed and the rest got themselves somehow out of danger. That night the Cronstadt sailors had to kill thirty soldiers. But they smashed the plot.

For days after that we could hear firing in all parts of Petrograd. A strange performance was going on. Beginning with the Winter Palace the sailors went systematically all over the city and finished the "booze" problem. They poured the wine on the streets or threw it into the canals. Cellars were flooded with it and pumped out with the aid of fire engines. The snow was rose stained and the city reeked with stale alcohol.

Groups of from ten to twenty sailors would come hurtling down the wide streets standing in a great motor-truck, armed and determined. "Another wine pogrom," the passerby would remark. It was a tremendous achievement; it kept the Russian revolution clean from the hideous guillotine days so characteristic of the French Revolution.

It was a miracle almost when one remembers that the sailors were hungry and cold and the wine would have warmed them—when one remembers even that the wine was worth millions of dollars.

While the sailors were severe with the thieves in Cronstadt they seemed to feel a certain reserve in dealing with them in Petrograd. If they found anything had been stolen that belonged to the people they would immediately go and reclaim it, administer a good scolding to the offender and depart.

The Alexandrinsky Rinok—Alexander Market—has another name in Petrograd. It is known as "Thieves' Market," because obviously most of the things that are for sale there are stolen goods. It is one of the most interesting places I ever visited. More antique treasures can be bought there than anywhere else except in old markets in Constantinople.

The range of loot is amazing. There are old Bokharas, ikons of wood, brass and iron, amber, carved silver chains, old enamel, cameos, tapestries, brocades, peasant embroideries, jewel-studded silver bracelets, heavy silver earrings and silver rings set with agates, old lusters, Bristol glass, Chinese porcelains, furs and great trays of precious and semi-precious stones. It is situated in a remote corner of Petrograd, and no guide-book ever mentions it. It seems to be entirely overlooked by tourists. I once took the American consul and Somerset Maugham, the playwright, to see it. The consul was shocked at the idea of such an open market for thieves, but like most foreigners, he decided to have no scruples, since it was not his country and was none of his business what peculiar customs alien peoples had. He found a pipe owned by Peter the Great, and Maugham picked up two marvellous bead purses.

After the Bolsheviki turned the Winter Palace into a people's museum they missed cases of table silver that had been stored in the cellar and was used at banquets. One afternoon the Cronstadt sailors surrounded the market and located all the missing articles. They scolded the merchants for their lack of loyalty to the revolution, but did them no violence.

The thieves themselves have peculiar twisted ideas of honour. An American friend of mine, returning from a political meeting at two in the morning, was held up by robbers. He thought for a minute and then said to them in his meagre Russian: *"Ya ne ponyemayo pa Russki; ya Americanets,"* which means: "I cannot understand Russian, I am American." The robbers were surprised. They consulted together and finally decided that it was unsportsmanlike to hold up a man who could not speak the language. So one of them said: "Well, go along, old fellow; we will get another one."

I told this story when I first came home, and one of the persons I told it to remarked quite seriously: "Of course, they were Bolshevik robbers." It was as absurd a thing to say as if you should go to Russia and tell a story about a hold-up in America and a Russian would remark: "Of course, they were Democrat or Republican robbers." We are so confused in this country by a mysterious yet effective and systematic discrediting of everything that has to do with the political party known as the Bolsheviki, that we are quite apt to make unintelligent comments of this kind.

When the telephone girls went on strike, at the instigation of the Cadets, after the November revolution, the Bolsheviki offered them higher wages and shorter hours, but, nevertheless, they haughtily refused. For more than a month the Cronstadt sailors took over the principal telephone exchanges and ran them as best they could. They never hesitated at any time to do anything that would aid the revolution. They carried coal to the factories to keep them going and to keep the workers from being out of work. They went on long expeditions into Siberia and brought back large supplies of flour to make bread for the army and feed the starving population. They are fighting to-day in Finland with the Red Guards against the Germans and the White Guards.

I am enough of a feminist to be pleased with the fact that the Cronstadt Soviet has been headed by a middle-aged woman for more than half a year. Her name is Madame Stahl, and she manages her many turbulent sons in a clear-headed and unperturbed manner.

Dubenko for a time fell from grace, as a result of his over-confidence in humanity. As head of the navy he was responsible for the retention of the higher command. Many high officers after a few months of Bolshevik rule, having evidently decided that the new government was going to stick, came back into the service. The common sailors were suspicious of them, but Dubenko believed them to be honest in their desire to aid Russia.

After the Brest-Litovsk negotiations and the subsequent German advance, it was discovered that these same high officers whom he had reinstated had betrayed part of the fleet. For example, they gave up the port of Narva without resistance to the Germans. Further investigation proved that they had held communication with the enemy through the diplomatic pouches. Dubenko was held responsible and was arrested, but was later released and exonerated.

On the opening day of the Third Congress of Soviets in Moscow in January, he married Alexandra Kollontay. This was one of the few romances among the revolutionary leaders.

CHAPTER XV

MARIE SPIRODONOVA

MARIE SPIRODONOVA looks as if she came from New England. Her puritanical plain black clothes with the chaste little white collars, and a certain air of refinement and severity about her seem to belong to that region more than to mad, turbulent Russia—yet she is a true daughter of Russia and of the revolution. She is very young—just past thirty—and appears exceedingly frail, but she has the wiry, unbreakable strength of many so-called "delicate" people, and great powers of recuperation.

Her early history as a revolutionist is exceptional even in the minds of the Russians, and they have grown used to great martyrs. She was nineteen when she killed Lupjenovsky, Governor of Tambov. Lupjenovsky had as dark a record as any official ever possessed. He went from village to village taking an insane, diabolical delight in torturing people. When peasants were unable to pay their taxes or offended him in any way at all, he made them stand in line many hours in the cold and ordered them publicly flogged. He arrested any one who dared hold a different political view from his own; he invited the Cossacks to commit all sorts of outrages against the peasants, especially against the women.

Spirodonova was a student in Tambov; she was not poor and she suffered no personal discomfort, but she could not bear the misery about her. She decided to kill Lupjenovsky.

One afternoon she met him in the railway station. The first shot she fired over his head to clear the crowd, the next she aimed straight at his heart, and Spirodonova has a steady hand as well as a clear head. Lupjenovsky was surrounded by Cossacks at the time. They arrested Spirodonova.

First the Cossacks beat her and threw her quite naked into a cold cell. Later they came back and commanded her to tell the names of her comrades and accomplices. Spirodonova refused to speak, so bunches of her long, beautiful hair were pulled out and she was burned all over with cigarettes. For two nights she was passed around among the Cossacks and the gendarmes. But there is an end to all things; Spirodonova fell violently ill. When they sentenced her to death she knew nothing at all about it, and when they changed the sentence to life imprisonment she did not know. She was deported to Siberia in a half-conscious condition. None of her friends ever expected to see her again.

When the February revolution broke out eleven

years later she came back from Siberia and offered her life again for freedom.

It is hard for us in comfortable America to understand the fervour of people like Spirodonova. It is a great pity that we do not understand it because it is so fine and unselfish. I once asked her how she managed to keep her mind clear during all the eleven years that she was in Siberia.

"I learned languages," she said.

"You see, it is a purely mechanical business and therefore a wonderful soother of nerves. It is like a game and one gets deeply interested. I learned to read and speak English and French in prison."

No other woman in Russia has quite the worship from the masses of the people that Spirodonova has. Soldiers and sailors address her as "dear comrade" instead of just ordinary "tavarish." She was elected president of the first two All-Russian Peasant Congresses held in Petrograd and she swayed those congresses largely to her will. Later she was chairman of the executive committee of the Peasants' Soviets and she is an extremely influential leader in the Left Socialist Revolutionist party.

When the Bolsheviki came into power they took over the land programme of the Socialist Revolutionists. This brought about great turmoil in the party. The Right maintained that it was their programme and no one had the right to steal it, but Spirodonova and all her wing only laughed.

"What difference does it make," she wanted to

know, "who gives the peasants their land—the principal thing is that they get it."

The first time I saw Spirodonova was at the Democratic Congress. Orators had been on the platform arguing about coalition for hours. A hush fell over the place when she walked on the stage. She spoke for not more than three minutes, giving a short, concise, clear argument against coalition. She began:

"*Krestian*—peasants—if you vote for coalition you give up all hope of your land!"

The great palace shook with the roaring protests of the proletariat against coalition when she ceased. Millions of peasants trust her implicitly and move with her judgment almost invariably. She has the greatest political following of any woman in the world.

If she were not such a clear thinker and so inspired a person, her leadership of the physical giants would be ludicrous. Spirodonova is barely five feet tall. She may weigh 100 pounds and she may weigh less. She has big grey eyes circled with blue rings, and soft brown hair which she wears in a coronet braid. She works on an average of about sixteen hours a day, and everybody in Russia pours into her office at 6 Fontanka to ask advice.

I used to go there and she would tell me interesting stories. One day I took in a Russian girl who belonged to the Menshevik party and who, therefore, was opposed to Spirodonova. She sat silent and listened to her for two hours. When we came out on the street the girl stopped and her eyes were full of tears.

"To think," she said, "that with such eyes and such a face she should ever kill a man! Until to-day I was her enemy—now I know she is the greatest woman in Russia!"

And to Spirodonova I wish also to make my salaam. I have not met a woman her equal in any country.

The last time I saw her she talked to me about the war and the possibility of a decent peace being secured at Brest-Litovsk. She had no faith in the success of the negotiations, and she was seriously working on what she called a "Socialist army." "We have made secret inquiries," she said, "and we know we will have enough men; they will all be volunteers; there must be no compulsion." I had a vision then of Spirodonova leading her peasant-soldiers to battle instead of through the intricate mazes of politics. . . .

She spoke sadly of the sabotagers, especially of the intellectuals. "They consider the Russian revolution an adventure and they hold aloof, but the Russian revolution is much more than that, even if it fails for the present. It is the beginning of social revolution all over the world; *it is social revolution here in full swing!* The whole country is taking part in it now. My reports come in from the remotest districts. The peasants are already conscious and are making social changes everywhere."

We talked about women and I wanted to know why more of them did not hold public office since Russia is the only place in the world where there is absolute sex equality. Spirodonova smiled at my question.

"I am afraid I will sound like a feminist," she confessed, "but I will tell you my theory. You will remember that before the revolution as many women as men went to Siberia; some years there were even more women. . . . Now that was all a very different matter from holding public office. It needs temperament and not training to be a martyr. Politicians are usually not very fine, they accept political positions when they are elected to them—not because they are especially fitted for them. I think women are more conscientious. Men are used to overlooking their consciences—women are not."

Angelica Balabanov, another Russian revolutionist, has much the same theory. She told me in Stockholm: "Women have to go through such a tremendous struggle before they are free in their own minds that freedom is more precious to them than to men." I wish I could believe it, but I can never see any spiritual difference between men and women inside or outside of politics. They act and react very much alike; they certainly did in the

Russian revolution. It is one of the best arguments I know in favour of equal suffrage.

Spirodonova as a member of the Left Socialist Revolutionist party is surrounded by a number of the finest young idealists in Russia. Hers is the only party that in a crisis rises above party for the benefit of the nation. It will have more and more to say as the revolution settles down.

The day I left Russia, Spirodonova gave me her picture. She hates publicity and it is the only photograph she ever gave to any one. . . . This one she tore off her passport but she refused to say good-bye. "You must come right back," she said, "when you have written your story. And never mind saying anything good about me, but do say something about the revolution. . . . Try to make them understand in great America how hard we over here are striving to maintain our ideals."

CHAPTER XVI

FROM ONE ARMY TO THE OTHER

THE Committee for Saving the Country and the Revolution with its usual disregard for facts, informed us one afternoon in the middle of November that Kerensky had rallied round him a huge army of Cossacks and was marching up from Tsarskoe Selo. The first train in that direction left about 6 P. M. We didn't know where it would land us, but we decided to take it anyway. There were three of us, all Americans.

The train jogged along without interruption. We fell into a discussion, and before we were aware we had travelled any distance at all the conductor came in and told us we were at Tsarskoe. Whether or not we had somehow crossed the lines from one army to the other we did not know, but we were uneasily aware of the fact that we carried only Bolshevik passes.

It was already dark and the town looked quite dead, with a single light flickering here and there. Around the station things looked normal enough— people were walking about and soldiers were standing guard. We asked one of the guards for the Commandant and he took us to a little office where

171

a ragged soldier sat writing. He looked up from
a pile of papers and gave us a weary smile.

"The station is still in the hands of the people,"
he said, when we told him we were reporters, "but
the Cossacks are just on the other side of the park
and I do not know how long we can hold. . . ."

"Can we wander through the town?"

"Certainly," he replied, "but do not attempt to
cross the park. One of our comrades was killed
there yesterday. She thought she could go over
and fraternise with the Cossacks. They shot her
just as she crossed the lines. . . ."

I verified this story after I returned to Petrograd. She had hoped to prevent the battle between the Red Guards and the Cossacks which took
place a few days later.

We were hungry and looked for the station restaurant. At one of the tables we found a lone
Englishman who commented on all our remarks by
one word, "Extraordinary!" which he drawled forth
in the proper British manner. When we got tired
of the monotony of his expression and stopped talking, a Russian soldier leaned over and whispered:
"Tell him something else, please. I want to hear
him say that word again. . . ."

We had cold fish and tea, then wandered through
the town. For blocks we did not see a soul. In
front of a large barn-like building we met a sailor
and a soldier. They seemed to be undecided
whether to go into the building or not. At last

one opened the door gingerly and a shaft of light came streaming through. We stopped also and looked in. A stout, well-dressed man was standing in the middle of the empty room. We decided from the rows of seats that it must be a small town theatre.

"Excuse me," said the sailor, "but will there be a performance to-night?"

The man on the inside bellowed with rage. "Performance!" he shouted. "Performance, with a battle at any moment? Your damned revolution, I tell you, has ruined my business!"

"Excuse me," said the sailor again, and shut the door.

We all stood there on the street for a moment. None of us knew just what to do. Then we showed our passes to the sailor and soldier expecting them to be friendly. They took the passes and looked them over solemnly and handed them back without a word. We felt sure that they must be anti-Bolshevik but what puzzled us was that they acted more afraid of us than we did of them.

A little further along we met a student and enquired the way to Ekaterina Palace. We walked slowly because it was moonlight and the pretty old town with its beautiful gold and white church was exquisite under the stars. Our route lay along the edge of the park and through the trees, now heavy with snow, we could see the camp-fires of the Cossacks. . . .

At the great iron entrance gate to the palace grounds we stopped to rest. On one side was a fountain built in the figure of a huge swan, from the mouth of which water gushed. We stood there laughing and talking until voices reached our ears. Looking up we saw sentries watching us from the wall; their bayonets shone ominously in the moonlight. We remembered the queer way the soldier and sailor had acted and we did not want to make another mistake, so this time we spoke to the sentries.

"What side are you on?" we asked officiously.

"We are neutral," they called down to us.

"We have business with the Commandant."

"Pass!"

And so we entered the great gates and came out on the broad road that encircles the palace. It is one of the loveliest old palaces in Russia. Huddled cosily on the top of a knoll, it rambles off in numerous ells and courts, as if it had been added to by each successive monarch. Nicholas II., after the 1905 revolution was afraid to come to Petrograd and spent much of his time in Ekaterinski.

We found the Commandant and his officers seated around a wood fire and we presented our passes. The Commandant looked concerned and consulted with several of his staff. Then he came back to us and said: "I am sorry to inform you that you have the wrong papers. It was dangerous. You might have been arrested. We are holding this place for Kerensky, but if you would like to go to the hotel to-night, I can issue an order so that you can secure a room and I will also give you correct passes and deny all knowledge of these. The battle will take place at four in the morning. . . ."

He ordered one of his aides to walk a little way with us into the town.

At the same time that we were stumbling around with the wrong passes, two other Americans, one a former preacher in Boston, turned revolutionist and Socialist, and one, the official interpreter for the American Red Cross mission in Petrograd, started to walk from their hotel in the city to the trenches of the Red Guard on the outskirts. They lost their way and pushed on through the mud for hours. The interpreter was a delicate chap with no stomach for battles. He had been entrusted with both passes which had been obtained at Smolny.

As they went along and darkness came upon them, they grew more and more nervous. The interpreter put the passes in his mouth for fear that they would encounter the Kerensky army and be searched. The passes were not very large and were made out on fine paper. At least that is the only way he can account for what happened—he swallowed the passes!

Shortly afterward they encountered the first Red Guard sentry. He demanded papers. They had none. So he chased them off towards Petrograd in the mud and rain and threatened them with violence if they ever came back again. In fact, the thing that hurt them most of all was that he told them he thought they were German agents. Americans, he remarked, wisely, do not usually speak Russian as fluently as the interpreter.

And while all this was going on we were presenting the wrong passes to the other side and being treated with great friendliness. Revolutions do not run along set formulas.

A few days later, after Kerensky's Cossacks were defeated, a huge procession marched through the streets of Petrograd to meet the returning Red Guards and soldiers. After standing all afternoon watching the demonstration, I went into a little restaurant on Zagorodny Prospekt. A very old and simple peasant came in and begged permission to blow on my fur coat to see if it were real seal. It is not seal, but he decided that it was. We began to talk and he asked me where I came from. I said that I was an American, and for some reason this seemed to excite him. He began to tell every one who entered about it.

I asked him curiously what he knew about America. For at least five minutes he was silent, thinking. Then he arose and gravely announced to the company: "America is a great nation! I know about America. Sewing machines come from America." Then he came over, kissed me on both cheeks, and gave me an apple and a dirty sandwich.

CHAPTER XVII

RED GUARDS AND COSSACKS

I WILL never forget the first time I saw the Red Guards going out to battle. A cruel wind swept the wide streets and hurled the snow against the bleak buildings. It was 25 degrees below zero; I felt ill with cold under my fur coat. And there they came, an amazing, inspired mass in thin, tattered coats and their pinched white faces—thousands and thousands of them! The Cossacks were marching on Petrograd and Petrograd rose to repel them. They came pouring out of the factories in a mighty, spontaneous *people's army*—men, women and children. I saw boys in that army not over ten years of age.

We were standing on the steps of the City Duma and one of the Duma members, a Cadet, said to me: "Look at the Hooligans. . . . They will run like sheep. Do you think such ragamuffins can fight?"

I didn't answer. I was thinking of many things, things way back that made up the deepest impressions of my childhood. For the first time I visualised Washington and his starving, ragged army at Valley Forge. . . . I felt suddenly that the revolution must live in spite of temporary military defeat, in spite of internal strife, in spite of everything. It was the Red Guards that made me realise that Germany will never conquer Russia in a hundred thousand years. . . .

I wish every one in America could have seen that army as I saw it—all out of step, in odds and ends of clothing, with all sorts of old-fashioned fighting implements—some only armed with spades. If that wish could be granted there would be much more sympathy and much less scorn for the Red army. It took infinite courage, infinite faith to go out untrained and unequipped to meet the traditional bullies of Russia, the professional fighters, the paid enemies of freedom. All of them expected to die. Suddenly they broke into a wailing, melancholy revolutionary song. I threw discretion to the winds and followed. . . .

Soldiers in the regular army used to have contempt for the workers in the towns—the soldiers are mostly peasants. They used to say that the people in the towns did all the talking, while they did all the fighting, but that was before the Red Guards came into being.

The city workers are smaller than the peasants; they are stunted and pale, but they fight like demons. Lately they have put up the most desperate resistance to the Germans in Finland and the Ukraine. In this particular battle with the Cossacks they were so unused to warfare that they for-

got to fire off their guns. But they did not know
the meaning of defeat. When one line was mowed
down another took its place. Women ran straight
into the fire without any weapons at all. It was
terrifying to see them; they were like animals pro-
tecting their young.

The Cossacks seemed to be superstitious about
it. They began to retreat. The retreat grew into
a rout. They abandoned their artillery, their fine
horses, they ran back miles. . . .

It was a strange procession that came back into
Petrograd the next day. A huge crowd went out
to meet them with the usual floating red banners,
singing the swinging new revolutionary songs.
The returning victorious army had been without
food for a long time and they were dead weary
but they were wild with joy. The tradition of
the Cossacks was broken! Never again should
they seem invincible to the people!

It is very necessary, if America and Russia are
ever going to enjoy the natural friendship that
they ought to enjoy that we in America understand
what the Red Guards, the Cossacks, the Tcheko-
Slovaks and other warring factions continually in
the public eye actually stand for.

The Red Guards are simply the rank and file of
the working people of the towns and cities. They
are not anarchists and they have a very construc-
tive tendency. They believe and fight for the

Soviet form of government. They are anti-German.

Most Americans know the history of the Cossacks, but there are interesting points upon which they are not at all informed. One of those points is—that the Cossacks have played very little part in the great war. No matter what opinion we have of Russia's failure in the end, we ought never to forget that she stood the brunt of the first years, that her casualties are the most appalling of any nation, estimated now at seven million. We must bear in mind that that seven million was composed mostly of *peasants*.

The Cossacks are really the cavalry branch of the army and, owing to the fact that virtually all the fighting is now done in the trenches, the Cossacks have not been called upon for heavy service. They have, consequently, had time and energy to be used in counter-revolutionary attempts. They have been of excellent assistance to the Germans by their co-operation with the rich bourgeoisie, for they have torn Russia with such dreadful internal strife that the revolutionists have had to waste as much precious energy in suppressing them as in repelling the invaders. It is because of such conditions that Soviet troops have been unable to hold a front and have had to sign a disgraceful peace which they must sooner or later break. But they cannot break it until they have rid themselves of such yokes and can re-organise their forces.

If the Cossacks were really as patriotic as they pretend it only seems reasonable that their course of action would have been quite different than it was. They would themselves have been so busy fighting the Germans that they would not have had time to add to the chaos in Russia. When we consider the Cossacks we have to face the fact that they have always been *paid* fighters; that they have shot down the Russian people at the command of the worst tyrants, without flinching. They are born and bred fighters and men of that sort do not usually die *for* revolution, but quite naturally oppose it. They are more comfortable under a militaristic régime; they would fit better under Prussian rule than under the democracy of the Soviet. With the death of militarism and the practical working out of the revolution they would have to seek other work.

But since the November Revolution the rank and file of the Cossacks have also revolted against their landlords and exploiters, and now have delegates in the Soviets, and are at least passive supporters of the Revolution.

Writing of civil war makes me think of a little incident that illustrates pretty well the attitude of many middle-class Russians at the present time. It was some time in December and the rich people were beginning to fear that the Soviet government was going to stick and were getting worried about it.

I had been invited to dinner at the home of a well-to-do Russian family. The hostess explained to me when I arrived that she was desolate because her cook had left. She gave her a salary of twenty rubles a month and at the present exchange that amounted to two dollars. The girl complained that, because she had to stand long hours in the bread-lines every day, she wore out her shoes. The cheapest shoes at the time cost one hundred and fifty rubles. If she saved every cent of her salary she could only buy one pair of shoes about every eight months, and rubbers were out of the question.

My hostess thought the girl was extremely unreasonable. "She ought to be beaten with a knout," she said.

At the table the talk drifted to politics. Every one began to malign the Bolsheviki. They said it would be wonderful if the Germans would only come in and take possession. There would be gendarmes on every corner and "dogs of peasants" running for their lives. . . .

I said I had a great deal of sympathy for the Bolsheviki because they seemed to be the only party with backbone enough to try to give the people what they wanted. My hostess sat up straight in her chair. "Why, my dear," she said, sincerely shocked, "you don't know at all what you are talking about. Why, my *servants* are Bolsheviki!"

They all expressed sorrow that the Cossacks seemed to be losing power.

"Anyway," remarked one woman, "you wouldn't be so stupid in America as to have a civil war."

I drew myself up with some pride. "Madam," I replied, "we had *the* Civil War."

So I was asked to explain. It was an odd experience. I thought the whole world knew. I told how many years it went on, how many were killed, what it was all about. When I began to talk about slavery and the position of the negroes my hostess began to beam with understanding. Suddenly she burst out: "Oh, yes, now I remember, and it is quite right that you should be nice to the negroes—they have such pretty songs!"

I was amused and at the same time depressed. This story is so typical. The middle class in Russia seem to know nothing of our Civil War, of their civil war or of the relations of such events. And they are extremely selfish. They will tell you that they want the Germans, or they want "law and order." What they really want is comfort at the cost of democracy and ideals.

Since the days of the November revolution the Red Guards have become steadily stronger and more efficient and the Cossacks have grown weaker. This was partly due to good politics on the part of the Bolsheviki. When they began to divide the land they said expressly in their decree—*this does not apply to Cossacks*. Now, there are great land owners in the Cossack regions as well as anywhere in Russia. There are rich and poor. An agitation for land began and it grew and grew until finally a delegation of Don Cossacks representing many thousands went to General Kaledin, Hetman of the Don Cossacks, and demanded that their land be divided after the manner of the Soviet government distribution. General Kaledin replied, "That will only happen over my dead body." Almost immediately his ranks deserted him, joining the Soviet. Kaledin, realising the hopelessness of his mistake, blew out his brains.

General Semionov was only recently chased out of Siberia, his men killing their officers and going over to the Bolsheviki. The backbone of the Cossack movement seems to be broken.

CHAPTER XVIII

THE RED BURIAL

I WENT to Moscow on the first train that entered the city after the Bolsheviki had won in the six days' fighting. It was difficult to find a place to sleep. I wandered from hotel to hotel. The stolid, bewhiskered clerks made odd replies to my queries.

"Yes," said one, "I have a large room on the top floor, but there are no panes in the windows. I hope the Barishna will not object."

It was twenty-five degrees below zero, so I continued my search. After about two hours I found a room at the National.

"It is extremely dangerous to be here," confided an Englishman I met in the hall who did not approve of "lady" war correspondents. "You will probably be murdered before morning."

My window looked out over the Kremlin and the Red Square. Night had already fallen. Out of the darkness loomed a long mysterious row of fires. I was able to move freely through the city as I had passes from both the Bolsheviki and the opposition. After dinner I walked over to investigate the fires.

The first thing I realised after I crossed under the great arch was that the Kremlin was still standing. We had had reports in Petrograd that it had been razed to the ground, but there it stood, beautiful beyond description, lit up weirdly by a long line of sputtering torches stuck upon poles beside the north wall.

As I came closer a strange sight unfolded before me. A huge trench, many hundreds of feet in length, was being carved out of the frozen ground. The tall figures of soldiers, the smaller and more gaunt figures of factory workers cast distorted silhouettes across the snow as they bent over their gruesome task.

A young student who read over my passes explained what they were doing. "They are digging the brotherhood grave," he said, "for the last martyrs of the revolution."

I stayed there nearly all night. It was terrifyingly still and lonesome. There was no sound but the clatter of spades and the sputter of torches; there were no stars and the darkness hung down heavily like a great bell.

I asked the soldiers why they had chosen this spot for the Red Burial. They said it was because they wished to bestow the greatest possible honour on their dead comrades and to bury them under the long row of linden trees, across from Our Lady of Iberia; and the fantastically lovely, many cu-

polaed Vasili Blazhanie showed their deep reverence. It is the holiest spot in all Russia.

About two o'clock I went with the student to the
Soviet, which had headquarters in a large building only a few blocks away. It hummed with
preparations for the funeral on the morrow. All
night long women and girls were sewing miles and
miles of red cloth, cutting and trimming and fash-
ioning it into banners for the procession. They
sewed with stern, set faces. Perhaps women knit-
ting under the guillotine wore some such expres-
sions. . . .

After arranging my permission to attend the
funeral we went back to the Red Square. The
trench by this time had become deep and long, and
the mounds beside it had grown into little hills.
About five o'clock we climbed stiffly over the edge
and straggled wearily home. The task was com-
pleted; the gaping hole was ready to receive five
hundred bodies.

I drank my tea and ate my black bread at the
hotel and got back to the Soviet at seven-thirty.
The procession began at eight. The Executive
Committee of the Soviet was to head the procession, and they kindly invited me to march with
them.

Feeling ran high that day and no one unknown
to the proletariat dared to venture out of doors.
All those with bad consciences—monarchists,
counter-revolutionists, speculators — hid behind

drawn blinds, afraid of a reign of terror. While only eight hundred people were killed in Moscow, it was a tremendously important battle; it marked the end of armed resistance by the upper classes; it was the last stand of the Junkers.

From early morning I stood on a mound of newly turned earth watching an immense sea of people pouring through the white, arched gateway of the old Tartar City—flooding all the Red Square. It was bitter cold. Our feet froze to the ground and our hands ached under our gloves. But the spectacle before us was so magnificent that we forgot everything else.

In by the gateway, out by the house of the Romanoffs, the crowd passed endlessly in one huge, interminable funeral procession. Slowly, rhythmically they moved along, like a great operatic pageant symbolizing the long, bitter struggle of the masses throughout the vast intricate fabric of history.

Fine looking young giants of soldiers wearing towering grey chapkies bore the rough wooden coffins, which were stained red as if in blood. After them came girls with shawls over their heads and round peasant faces, holding large wreaths of artificial flowers that rattled metallically as they walked. Then there were bent old men and bent old women and little children. There were cavalry regiments and military bands and people carrying enormous banners that floated out in long, red waves over the heads of the crowd.

Great banners had been suspended from the top of the wall and reached down to the earth. On all the banners were inscriptions about the revolution and the hopes of the workers. Above the high red wall the golden domes of the four old churches inside the Kremlin shone out dizzily against the pale sky. The dark Bell Tower and the house of Boris Gordunoff seemed to be frowning.

All the churches and all the shrines were closed. How impressive it was! No ceremony, no priests; everything so simple and so real!

Sometimes the Lettish band would start suddenly to play the funeral hymn and the soldiers, sailors, the Red Guards and even the little boys and old men would take off their hats; the snow coming down in big flakes fell on their bowed heads, like a benediction. Troops of cavalry rode by at full salute. The martial note of the hymn stirred our blood and the wailing, Oriental notes were full of hopeless sorrow. . . .

Women all around began to sob and one quite near me tried to hurl herself after a coffin as it was being lowered. Her thin coating of civilisation dropped from her in a moment. She forgot the revolution, forgot the future of mankind, remembered only her lost one.

With all her frenzied strength she fought against the friends who tried to restrain her. Crying out the name of the man in the coffin, she screamed, bit, scratched like a wounded wild thing until she was finally carried away moaning and half unconscious. Tears rolled down the faces of the big soldiers.

Sometimes the procession varied by the appearance of a great untrained chorus singing the Revolutionary Funeral Song. No people in the world sing together as well as the Russians; no people love so to express themselves by song. The chorus rose and swelled, rich and resonant in the thin winter air—like a great organ in some fine old cathedral.

Twilight began to settle, softening everything. The sky grew warmer and the snow took on a rosy tint. All the wreaths had been hung in the trees and they swayed back and forth like strange, multicoloured fruit. It was seven o'clock when the last coffin was lowered and the dirt began to be shovelled in.

I had other acquaintances in Moscow—a merchant family turned speculator since the war. They had invited me for dinner and the table groaned with food. The warmth and light of the room stunned me after the thin bitterness of the Red Square.

The three sons of this family were all fit for military service, but had bribed their way free. All three carried on illegal businesses. One somehow managed to get gold from the Lena gold mines to mysterious parties in Finland. One gambled in food. One owned a controlling interest in a chocolate factory which furnished the co-operative stores on condition that the co-operatives first supply his family with everything he wanted. So, while people starved just around the corner, they had an abundance of everything. And they were charming and cultured and very pleasant to their friends. . . .

While we were at the table the talk turned to the Red Burial and then to the army. One of the men showed me a pitiful appeal sent out to the rich families by the Moscow Soviet, begging for shoes and clothes for the soldiers at the front. The company laughed uproariously; they said they would burn their clothes before they would give them to the proletariat. I couldn't help thinking of the people at home, of my own brothers fighting in France, and how quickly we would have answered such an appeal, and I was shocked at the difference. No wonder there is such class bitterness in Russia!

A discussion of the Germans followed and most of the company expressed themselves in favour of a German invasion. Just for a test I asked them to vote on what they really would rather have— the soldiers' and workers' government or the Kaiser. All but one voted in favour of the Kaiser.

I rode home at midnight in a jingling sleigh across the Red Square. It was silent and deserted.

CHAPTER XIX

IT is impossible to compare the French Revolutionary Tribunal with the Russian Revolutionary Tribunal without being struck at once by the complete dissimilarity of the two institutions. No institution could be a more definite expression of revolutionary thought or a more faithful indicator of the character of a people than a revolutionary tribunal. The principal business of the French court was to sentence suspected persons to death by the guillotine. During the whole time I was in Russia and watched this extraordinary body at work, not one person was sentenced to death.

I think of two characteristic cases.

The first was the case of Countess Panina. When the Bolsheviki came into power Panina had in her possession ninety thousand rubles belonging to the government. She refused to turn it over to the new authorities because she wanted to hold it until the Constituent Assembly; she refused to recognise the claims of the Soviet government. So she was arrested and held in Peter and Paul Fortress.

When her trial came up it made a notable stir. The courtroom was packed with a motley crowd, workers, reformers, monarchists. Most of the sessions were held in the new palace of Nicholai Nicholaiovitch. It was a circular, dead-white room with red hangings and looked curiously like a stiff modern stage set. At a long mahogany table with a red and gold cover sat the seven judges. Jukoff, a workman, was the president. Two of the judges wore the uniforms of private soldiers. The first day they looked a little embarrassed, but on all occasions maintained a surprising poise and dignity.

The first person to speak in the defence of Countess Panina was an old workman who was grateful to her for various reasons. He arose and said that she had brought light into a life which once knew only darkness. "She has given me the possibility to think," he said. "I could not read and she taught me to read. Then she was strong and we were weak. Now she is weak and we (the masses) are strong. We must give her her liberty. The world must not hear that we are ungrateful and that we imprison the weak." As he spoke he grew more and more emotional until he finally emitted a weird, hysterical shriek. "I cannot bear to see her sitting here a prisoner!" he cried and, weeping loudly, he left the room.

Paid lawyers did not make a particular impression at these trials; technical points mattered not in the least. Countess Panina's smart lawyer bored his audience frightfully. The last speaker was a fiery young boy from one of the Petrograd factories. He could not have been more than eighteen years of age. He said in effect:

"Let us not be sentimental. Panina is not a countess here, she is a plain citizen, and she has taken the people's money. We do not want to harm her—to do her any injustice. All we ask is that she return the money.

"The old man is grateful that she taught him to read. We live in a new age now. We do not depend on charity for 'light.' We believe that every man has the right to an education. With money such as Panina is keeping from the people we shall found schools, where every one shall learn. As revolutionists we do not believe in charity, we are not grateful for chance crumbs that fall from the tables of the rich."

Following his plea the court adjourned, and after a few minutes came back with this decision: Countess Panina shall remain in Peter and Paul Fortress until she returns the people's money. At the moment she complies with this demand she will be given her full liberty and *she shall be turned over to the contempt of the people.*

Panina decided at once to relinquish the funds. In almost any other country in such tense times they would have killed Panina, especially since she was one of the chief sabotagers against the new

régime. With her experience she could have been
of great assistance, but she did everything possible
to wreck the proletarian government.

Another trial held in the Wiborg quarter of
Petrograd and presided over by two men and one
woman illustrates the treatment of petty cases.
This time the court was packed with working people. The case concerned a poor man who had
stolen money from a woman news vendor. The
court questioned the man, and he rose up to defend
himself.

"I was feeling very sad," he said. "I was tired
of walking around the dark, cold streets. I thought
if I could only go into a warm place where there
were lights and people laughing I would be happy.
I thought of Norodny Dom and I thought I would
like to go there and hear Tchaliapin."

"Why did you decide to steal from this particular woman?" asked the court.

"I thought a long time," explained the man. "I
was standing on the corner of a street watching
her sell her papers. She sold to many rich people
—enemies of the poor—and I decided that in a
way she herself was a monarchist and a capitalist.
Did she not handle their papers as well as ours?
So I took her money. And for three days she did
not find me."

The court meditated for some minutes and
finally one of the judges asked very solemnly, "Did
you feel better after you had been to the theatre?"

Russians are truly marvellous. Not one person in the court laughed at that question. The thief replied that he did feel better. He said that it was impossible not to be lifted up by such fine singing.

The news vendor made a plea for herself. She maintained that she was not by any means a capitalist, but a person of real service to the community. She was a revolutionist, she believed in free speech and therefore she thought it only just that she give out all the news from all sides.

The court adjourned. When they came back they announced that they believed the argument of the woman to be fair and just. The argument of the man to be unjust, therefore the man should in some way reimburse the woman for what he had taken from her. They told the audience that it could decide what the man should give after explaining that the man had no money.

Everybody consulted in excited little groups and after an hour reached this decision: The man should give his goloshes (rubbers) to the woman. They were worth approximately the same amount as the money he had taken. The woman was entirely satisfied, as she said she was without goloshes and it was necessary for her to stand on the wet streets all day. The man was entirely satisfied because he said that it relieved his conscience. He shook hands with the woman and they were friends. Every one went home smiling.

It sounds like a funny story unless one thinks about it, then it gives one quite another feeling. Justice, if it is justice at all, has to be simple. In the complicated laws of highly civilised countries we have pretty well forgotten about real justice; we depend on tricks, alibis, technicalities, evasions of all sorts. The Russian laws were particularly bad. The Soviet government decided to re-build the whole business and in the meantime they established the revolutionary tribunal. It was never the intention of any of the parties in power to continue indefinitely this crude justice.

In Petrograd I knew a number of women lawyers. One was the young sister of Evreimov, the playwright. Natalie Evreimov was the first woman secretary to a Convention of Justices, which in Russia was a regular formal court of three judges to consider small cases. She had worked a year before the courts were abolished and she was furious with the Soviets. This group of women lawyers were all liberals, but they were impatient to be practising and had great contempt for the simple justice being dealt out by the tribunal.

One evening I went to an entertainment at the house of one of them. My hostess had on a ring that reminded me of America. It was a plain gold band with enameled English letters. When I enquired about it, my hostess blushed and told me a story. "It was given to me by an American business man," she said. "He was then my fiancé. I was seventeen and he was forty. He could not stand the frivolity of a young Russian girl. I was continually teasing him and making his life a burden, so he returned to America and I never heard of him again. The ring is very mysterious. For years I have pondered on the meaning of the letters. I once asked him to explain the meaning, but he said he was bound not to tell."

She slipped the ring from her finger and I read in astonishment, "I. O. O. F." And I didn't have the heart to disillusion her.

CHAPTER XX

THE FOREIGN OFFICE

NO foreign office in the world ever could be like the Bolshevik Foreign Office; there were strange new departments and strange activities which didn't fit at all with the old-time servants in their formal blue uniforms with brass buttons and red collars, who took off the hats and rubbers of the common soldiers with the same outward show of politeness that they once abjectly displayed towards Grand Dukes and Ambassadors. Every one called every one else "comrade" and the clerks sold revolutionary pamphlets, which they kept on long tables in the corridors.

Trotsky rarely came to the Foreign Office, but did all his business at Smolny and the *svetzars* were kept busy running errands between the two institutions. Dr. Zalkin his assistant, had charge of the details of the work. He is a handsome man with a great shock of grey hair and a young face; he speaks four languages and holds many university degrees. On his desk was always some scientific work, usually French, which he read in spare moments. He appeared to be masquerading in workman's clothes, because he looked so aristocratic with his long, delicate face, slender build and sensitive hands. Nevertheless, he was one of the sincerest revolutionists that I knew.

To an American, accustomed to the time-clock and high speed, all the offices seemed to be run in an incredibly haphazard fashion. There was the ante-room of the minister's cabinet where foreigners came to get their passports stamped. The fee was fifteen rubles, unless you could prove you were a member of the working class. When I took my passport in to have it viséd, my money was handed back and the clerk remarked, with a smile, "In my opinion a reporter is truly a member of the proletariat."

Perhaps the most interesting of all the departments was the Department of War Prisoners, which was particularly active during the month or two after the last Revolution. What grand plans for a revolt in the Central Empires were hatched in those days! What magnificent hopes to end the war, to bring peace to the world by a rising of the workers! Mentsikovski was Commissar of the bureau.

Next door was the newly founded Bureau of International Revolutionary Propaganda, under the head of Boris Reinstein of Buffalo, New York, where also worked two other American Socialists, John Reed and Albert Rhys Williams. The business of the Committee, among other things, was to carry revolutionary ideas into Germany and Austria by every means possible. Reed and Williams introduced American advertising psychology—briefness and concrete impressions—into the propaganda. They got out, for example, an illustrated edition of *Die Fackel*. They reproduced a picture of the old German Embassy in Petrograd with the caption: "German soldiers and workers—Why don't you put a German workman in this place?"

They inserted pictures of revolutionists tearing down the royal insignia with the comment: "When workmen are blind they reverence such symbols. When will you tear the mask from your eyes?"

There was an illustration showing a group of workmen sitting around comfortably in a palace. "Workers have always built the palaces," read the caption, "and have defended them with their blood, now for the first time they live in the palaces they built and defended. Why do you lag behind?"

The Americans added energy to the plans of the Russians. Every day they saw that tons of revolutionary literature were placed on the trains and started towards the front. Williams even formed a Foreign Legion to help repel the threatened invasion.

There was the Department of the Press, under the direction of Radek. These three departments published jointly newspapers in three languages—in German, *Die Fackel;* Hungarian, *Nemzetzkoi Socialista;* and Roumanian, *Inainte.* The papers were distributed extensively along the enemy fronts, smuggled over the lines and circulated in prison camps. The Germans are master propagandists and they know too well its value and wrecking ability not to be alarmed by it. It is worth noting that President Wilson's various messages were always smuggled into Germany in this way. . . .

Secret meetings were held in the Foreign Office, where German and Austrian prisoners came to plot revolution in their own countries. I was the only woman ever present. We had to sign our names when we went in, as if we were making a death pact and it was truly a dangerous business. Whoever signed was somehow discovered and thenceforth marked by both the monarchists and their co-workers, the German agents. Russians used to say to me jokingly and half in warning, "You have a blonde spy following you to-day," or "I know your spy—he's one of the Black Hundred."

At first I didn't mind; it was a new experience. But it soon got on my nerves. A weird, emaciated little man came several times to see me and claimed to be an American. He invited me to come to his house. After I told him I knew he was a spy he ceased coming, but daily my papers were gone over. I left my place on Troisky Ulitsa after the editor of *Novia Jisn,* Gorky's paper, told me I was followed by one of the most notorious of the Tsar's secret police. I took up headquarters in the As-

toria Hotel, which was the official war hotel.
There I was not molested because it was impossible to go in and out without a pass unless one
was known. Husky Cronstadt sailors guarded the
entrance.

Two weeks after I went to live in the Astoria
I was followed by two spies into the Tauride Palace. They got in, but they could not get out. The
Lettish guards held them and took away their note-
books. All they contained were exact statistics of
my comings and goings, the number of times I
took carriages, street-cars, and how long I stayed
at various places. I must have been a disappointing subject because I never even took part in a
discussion; I was only allowed as an observer. The
Bolsheviki let my spies cool their heels in Peter
and Paul for over a month, then let them go, as
they do most every one else they arrest, on the
promise to seek honest employment.

The Foreign Office faces the Winter Palace and
the architecture and the colour conform to that of
the greatest palace in the world. One room where
the prisoners used to meet was extremely beautiful,
furnished in massive mahogany and old brocades.
Nothing ever discouraged me as much as the conduct of the German soldier prisoners at these meetings. The representatives of the small nationalities of Austria-Hungary were violent revolutionists;
they acted much as the Russians did. That is, they
came in, in their old clothes and muddy boots, and

sat down quite at ease amid all the splendour. The Russians have come to the conclusion that the palaces are theirs and therefore they ought to utilise them and that is all there is to it. Not so the German privates. They entered timidly, sat on the edges of their chairs, twirled their caps nervously in their big awkward fingers. . . .

One night a Prussian officer wedged in on false pretences. He had lied to the prisoners, pretended to be a revolutionist, and had been sent as a delegate. He sat glowering at the company until he was asked point-blank for his opinion. Then he confessed he was only posing as a revolutionist because he had suspected what was going on. He was ejected without further ceremony.

As soon as he was out of the room all the German privates began to talk at once. They said that they were for the revolution, that they believed in it, and wanted to help in every possible way. They were against their government, but they were afraid to speak while the officer was in the room. Officers in camp had told them, they confessed, that they would all be shot when they returned to Germany. . . .

One of the Russians leaned forward and spoke quietly. "Comrade," he said, "how many officers have you got in your camp?"

"Why," answered the soldier, "just a few—just three or four."

"Why don't you kill them, comrade?" the Russian went on in his even voice.

For a moment the German soldiers were dumbfounded. They looked at each other in blank astonishment, whether because they were horrified or because the idea had never before occurred to them, I do not know. At last one of them spoke very slowly—every word came out as if it hurt him all over.

"Yes," he said, "you are right. It must come to that. If we kill them we will no longer have them to fear."

The Russian spoke kindly, as a doctor speaks to a sick child. "Remember," he soothed, "we also were afraid of our officers. Your officers and our officers stand for the same sort of tyranny. We do not fear our officers any more. We are free now."

The Germans agreed solemnly, but their faces were dead white. One caused a ripple of laughter from the Russians when he said, "It is true that we shall have revolution—but *wir mussen orden haben.*"

For a moment I caught a vision of that orderly, mechanical, thorough, inevitable German revolution. So many heads a minute, no forgiveness, no compromise. Order can be more deeply horrible than the utmost confusion. And yet I suppose it is the only way—a complete reckoning, a calm, final judgment. . . .

So far the German social-democrats have been disappointing in the mass. They have not risen to the point other socialists expected them to. Perhaps it is because they have so much to overcome; the step is far greater for them. And yet there are everywhere signs of a good start—the mutiny in the fleet, the strikes starting in Vienna and spreading all over Germany, the latest evidences of Austria's discontent. . . . In the German advance volunteer troops from other fronts were used because the German officers did not trust the men impregnated with Bolshevik propaganda. German prisoners at Pskof helped the Red Guards to retake the city. They are changed after living in Russia. I once heard an Austrian officer speaking to a group of prisoners. "How can we stand by," he asked them, "and allow our government to crush the Russian revolution? We are sick of war, but if we are men we must fight with our Russian brothers."

While the negotiations were going on at Brest-Litovsk the prisoners' delegates met and passed the following resolution:

"The Russian revolution is playing the part of all oppressed nations and classes against all tyranny and exploitation. The Russian Revolution remained true to itself when its representatives summed up the peace conditions.

"This appeal is in the name of the Germans from Germany, of the Germans from Austria, the

Hungarians, the Bohemians, Slovenians, the Roumanians, the Croatians, the Serbians and other nationalities. The war prisoners of these nationalities accept unreservedly the peace proposition of the Russian government. If it should turn out that the government of Carl of Austria and Wilhelm of Germany refuse to conduct the peace negotiations on the ground of the above propositions, then we, the Germans, Hungarians, etc., immigrants and war prisoners declare war on the German and Austro-Hungarian imperialists, and we will fight in the trenches shoulder to shoulder with our Russian comrades, because the further conduct of engaging in such a war means a revolution aiming at the emancipation of entire mankind, and we know how to discharge our duties as revolutionists. At the same time we appeal to the German and Austro-Hungarian comrades in the trenches fighting under the banners of the German, Austro-Hungarian imperialists to sabotage the war, to surrender themselves, and come over to the side of the Russian revolutionist army, and to do all they can to disorganise the forces of those imperialist governments.

"We appeal to the masses of Germany and Austria-Hungary to develop a strong revolutionary movement against their governments, and we call upon our fellow-workers, men and women, engaged in the war industries in those countries to sabotage their work. They must not prepare any more ammunitions for those governments because that ammunition will be used now, not against their enemies, but against their own fathers, brothers and sons, fighting for international democracy and solidarity, because from now on we, the Germans, Austrians, Hungarians, etc., will be fighting in the Russian trenches."

In order to explain better to the masses and the soldiers of the Central Powers, the appeal designated broadly what the Russian revolution gave to the Russian people, and what it aimed to give. It also demanded that the oppressed nations in Austria-Hungary, etc., be allowed a referendum on the question of self-definition, and that all soldiers, gendarmes, officials, be removed and complete freedom of such a referendum be secured. This resolution was telegraphed to Trotsky at Brest.

I cannot help but feel, after my close glimpses of the revolutionists of Russia, that if Germany tries to absorb Russia she will soon suffer from a mighty attack of national indigestion from which she will not be able to recover. Revolution is an insidious disease, spreading under tyranny, flourishing under autocracy. . . .

CHAPTER XXI

WOMEN SOLDIERS

NO other feature of the great war ever caught the public fancy like the Death Battalion, composed of Russian women. I heard so much about them before I left America that it was one of the first things I investigated when I got to Russia. In six months I saw them go through a curious development which divided them into two bitter hostile camps. Their leader, Leona Botchkarova, was severely beaten and had to be taken to a hospital. Hurt, uncomprehending, she declared: "I do not want to be associated with women! I do not trust them!" If she had been a thinker as well as a fighter she would have known that sex had little to do with the matter. Class struggle permeated everything and it hurled the women's regiments into the maelstrom with everything else.

Near Smolny Institute there was a recruiting station. It was here that I made my first friends among the women soldiers. A short dumpy little girl with cropped black hair stood awkwardly holding a big gun with a long bayonet. She regarded me belligerently.

"Stoi! What do you want?" she queried. I decided she must be the guard and explained my mission.

Inside were half a dozen girls sitting on stools in the hallway. They were arrayed in the strangest attire; one had on dancing slippers and a frivolous waist; another high-heeled French shoes, and still another wore brown buttoned shoes and green stockings—the only universal note was short hair and men's trousers.

They looked like the chorus of a comic opera in various stages of make-up. They all began to talk to me at once, as is the Russian custom. "Who are you?" "Are you English or American?" "Are you going to join the regiment?"

A very intelligent and lovely girl by the name of Vera, who was in charge that day, came out and invited me into her office. I often went back after that and had lunch with her. She was well read and spoke five languages. The only thing I didn't like about her was that she loved to salute so much that she kept doing it all the time, and as she was the superior officer, she couldn't very well salute any one else but me. This I found very droll after coming from France, where war correspondents are not treated like commanders-in-chief.

Vera explained about the variety of shoes. She said that they had ordered boots, but had never heard any further word. There was a very good reason, which I found out afterwards; there was no leather. The only women soldiers that ever did get boots or overcoats or anything else they needed were the first recruits to the Death Battalion. All the others were "just waiting" as every one does in Russia.

It was the Death Battalion that took part in the last Russian offensive. There were two hundred and fifty in the battle; six were killed and thirty wounded. That was their last and only battle, except for the girls who were brought to the Winter Palace the day that it fell. And they surrendered before a single one was wounded.

I gathered these statistics very carefully and have compared them with the statistics gathered by reliable persons. I took great pains because I could not believe them when I first got them. I had been led to believe that the movement was much larger. In all Russia less than three thousand were gathered into the recruiting stations. It is interesting to note that many more have since taken part in the Red Guard Army.

Women in Russia have always fought in the army. In my opinion the principal reason for the failure of the woman's regiment was segregation. There will always be fighting women in Russia, but they will fight side by side with men and not as a sex. Botchkarova herself fought several years before she organised the Death Battalion at the instigation of Kerensky and Rodzianko.

When the Soviet formally took over the govern-

ment the women soldiers were given two months'
leave. The majority were ordered home and told
to put on female attire because they were considered enemies of the revolution. There was a good
deal of misunderstanding on both sides.

I came across a peculiar case. I had heard a
rumour that some of the girls had been mistreated
the night the Winter Palace fell. I didn't believe
it, but I wanted to assure myself. After a great
deal of searching around I found that one girl
really had been hurt and had been in a hospital.
And another girl had committed suicide because
she was "disappointed in her ideals." I got the
address of the girl who had been sick and went
round to see her.

She lived with another girl in one of the great
barnlike unused buildings so common in Petrograd.
Kira Volakettnova was her name. She was a
dressmaker and had always been very poor. The
building had a court with snow piled high in the
centre. Garbage and filth of all sorts were thrown
on top of the snow.

I knocked a long time at the front door; nobody
answered. I found the back door wide open and
went in. Hearing a noise in one of the rooms, I
called out but received no reply. I opened the
door and a lot of startled chickens ran in every
direction. I searched all over that floor with no
result, and finally went to the second floor. There
in a tiny room I found Kira and her friend, Anna

Shub. Anna was seventeen and came from Moghilev.

I asked Kira to explain how she was hurt.

"Well, that night when the Bolsheviki took the Winter Palace and told us to go home, a few of us were very angry and we got into an argument," she said.

"We were arguing with soldiers of the Pavlovsk regiment. A very big soldier and I had a terrible fight. We screamed at each other and finally he got so mad that he pushed me and I fell out of the window. Then he ran downstairs and all the other soldiers ran downstairs. . . . The big soldier cried like a baby because he had hurt me and he carried me all the way to the hospital and came to see me every day."

"And how do you live now?" I said. "How do you manage to get enough to eat?"

Anna Shub answered my question. "Why, the Red Guard," she said, blushing a little, "have been dividing their bread with us, and yesterday," she went on proudly, "they brought us six pieces of wood, and so we have been warm all day."

"Have you forgiven the Bolsheviki for disarming you?" I asked Kira.

Anna Shub broke in and asked excitedly: "Why should *we* forgive *them?* It is they who should forgive us. We are working girls and traitors have been trying to persuade us to fight our own people. We were fooled and we almost did it."

"How was that?" I asked.

Anna reached under her cot and took out a pasteboard box. The contents of that and what she had on her back was all that she had in the world besides a sick sparrow. The sick sparrow she had picked up on the street half frozen. Now it hopped about the room looking for crumbs and picking at spots on the floor. Anna opened the box and took out some folded papers. Two were small posters like those pasted daily on the buildings on the streets of Petrograd. "Read them," she said. They were written in the usual extravagant and colourful language of Russian bulletins. I give a free translation:

"Come with us in the name of your fallen heroes! Come with us and dry the tears and heal the wounds of Russia. Protect her with your lives.

"Wake up and see clear, you who are selling the heads of your children to the Germans. Soon, very soon, you will prefer to face ten German bayonets to one tigress. We pour out our maledictions upon you. Enough words! It is time to take up arms. Only with a storm of fire will we sweep the enemy off Russian soil. Only with bayonets will we attain a permanent peace. Forward against the enemy! We go to die with you."

After I finished reading Anna went on with her story.

"I left home," she said. "I left everything because I thought the poor soldiers of Russia were tired after fighting so many years, and I thought we ought to help them. When I arrived in Petrograd I began to see the truth; we were supposed to be shaming the soldiers."

Tears welled in her eyes. "I felt as if I myself could die of shame. I didn't know what to do. And then, just before the Winter Palace fell, one of the aristocrats of the Death Battalion came in and asked us to go down and join the Cossacks to fight the revolution."

"I am a Jew," said Anna, "and I come from within the Pale. Liberty is dearer than life to me. And I . . . I was actually asked to do this thing!"

"I used to talk to the people in the bread-line," she went on, "about the Bolsheviki, and they said they were not bad people, and that they were our friends. When you go back to America," she said eagerly, as if every one would know about her unfortunate conduct, "tell them I am a woman soldier, and I fight only imperialistic invaders."

Anna and Kira had virtually no clothes at all. They had thin summer clothing, pieced out with all sorts of rag-tags they had managed to gather together, and they didn't know where to get their next meal. I offered them money and clothes. At first they both wept and refused and then they were quite happy in accepting.

A few nights before I left Petrograd I stopped at one of the huge military hospitals, where women soldiers were working. The Bolsheviki had secured them places so that they could get enough to eat. . . . That very day I had seen two begging at one of the stations. I found that the girls had already gone home for the night. Following vague directions I walked up a dark street for about a quarter of a mile. The little house where they stayed stood in the middle of a deserted garden, snow-covered and desolate.

I went through an open door that sagged down on a broken hinge, and felt my way along the hall until I saw a shaft of light. I knocked and entered. Inside the little room was a peasant, his wife, their baby, the stove, the bed and a highly pungent odour of cooking cabbage.

At the next door I had better success. This time it was a large room containing ten girls and ten beds, a long bench and a Russian stove. They were delighted to have company, especially from "so far away." We sat down on the bench and talked most of the night. Their stories were much the same as Anna's.

"We are girls from little towns," said one. "Some of us came with our parents' blessing, but most of us came with their curses. We were all moved by a high resolve to die for the revolution.

"How unhappy we have been! Everywhere we have been misunderstood. We expected to be honoured, to be treated as heroes, but always we were treated with scorn. On the streets we were insulted. At night men knocked at our barracks and cried out blasphemies. Most of us never got within miles of the front. The soldiers thought we were militarists and enemies of the revolution, and at last they disbanded us and took our arms away."

Another girl began to talk.

"That night," she said, "all of us thought of suicide; there was nothing left. We had no clothes and nowhere to go; life was unbearable. Some of us wanted to appeal to the Bolsheviki, to have a conference with them and explain our purpose. We wanted them to know that we would go to the front and fight for them or for any party. Our aim was to save Russia. But when we suggested that there were members of our battalion who objected and tried to get us to go down and join the Cossacks. We were horrified. We understood then how we had been misled. Of course we would not go. . . ."

"Thirteen went," cried one of the girls.

"But they were aristocrats," answered the first speaker in great contempt.

They were violent in their denunciation of Botchkarova. "She calls us cowards," they said, "but it is she who runs away. It is she who abandons her country, who believes neither in Russian women nor Russian men. . . ."

It was just about the time that the negotiations were broken off at Brest-Litovsk and the possibility of the German advance was in everybody's mouth. I asked them if they would offer their services to the Soviet government in that case. They replied unanimously that they would.

"And how about you?" said one. "Will you fight with us?"

I said that I would. The idea pleased them very much. I was on my way home when the advance began and could not keep my word. But perhaps there will still be opportunity. Russia will be at war with Germany until the present German government is overthrown, and in that struggle for freedom of the Russian people I offer my services unreservedly.

It was almost dawn when I bid the women soldiers farewell. One of them walked a little way with me into the night. It was painfully cold.

"Be sure to come back," she urged sweetly as we shook hands.

"I give you my word of honour," I said, feeling terribly solemn. I looked down and suddenly I realised that her feet were bare. . . .

When I think back now she personifies Russia to me, Russia hungry and cold and barefoot—forgetting it all—planning new battles, new roads to freedom.

CHAPTER XXII

FREE SPEECH

A NUMBER of papers were shut down after the November revolution and the conservatives wagged their heads with a good deal of reason and said: "Well, you see how it is when the radicals come into power—they do the same things that we do." It was true and not true. In the first place, the Soviet government does not pretend to believe that the reactionaries should be allowed to control the press, that a handful of capitalists should make public opinion. They believe that the press should be the expression of the people as well as the government. . . .

There was a great scarcity of paper in Russia and they argued that a just arrangement would be to limit the amount of press-paper, ink, etc., to the proportion of votes cast by each political party. A decree was passed to this effect which cut down the papers of the conservatives to a large extent.

Another reason for suppression was that many papers refused to obey the new advertising laws, making advertising a government monopoly. This law was passed in order to obtain funds for running the government and maintaining the army.

During the intenseness of the insurrection certain papers were stopped because they attempted to create panic and incited to riot by printing all sorts of exaggerated reports. An explanation of steps taken to combat this is given by Lenine in the *Decree of the Press,* which was passed by the Petrograd Soviet. It said in part:

"In the serious, decisive hour of the revolution and the days immediately following, the Provisional Revolutionary Committee was compelled to adopt a whole series of measures against the counter-revolutionary press of all shades.

"At once cries arose from all sides that the new socialistic authority was violating the essential principles of its programme. The Workers' and Soldiers' Government draws attention to the fact that in our country behind such a shield of liberalism is hidden an attempt to poison the minds and bring confusion into the consciousness of the masses. It was impossible to leave such a weapon as wilful misrepresentation in the hands of the enemy, for it is not less dangerous than bombs and machine guns.

"That is why temporary and extraordinary measures have been adopted for cutting off the stream of calumny in which the yellow press would be glad to drown the young victory of the people.

"As soon as the order will be consolidated, all administrative measures against the press will be suspended. Full liberty will be given within the broadest and most progressive measures in this respect; even in critical moments the restriction of the press is admissible only within the bounds of necessity."

It is possible for papers to exist in Russia without advertisements because the price of a newspaper is very high and they are only two-page affairs with no illustrations. The editors never heard of a "human interest" story. Papers are not delivered, except foreign papers. News vendors are sold out an hour after the papers appear on the streets, there being always the greatest hunger for news.

The most important official notices, since the revolution, were pasted on the walls of buildings or printed on handbills and distributed throughout the city.

The advertising decree was interesting; it included an elaborate plan for state control. Offenders of this law were promised three years' imprisonment, but no editor was ever sentenced, although many were convicted. The usual procedure was to close up the paper for a week and then allow it to reappear under another name.

A number of well-known Russian writers got out one issue of a paper called *Journal Protest,* with articles in it denying the right, under any circumstances, of suppression of the press. Among the contributors were Korolenko, Sologub, Kirakoff, Max Mijoneff, Professor Kiraieff and Eu-

gene Zamiatin. The protest did not create any noticeable effect on public opinion and after one attempt was given up.

Zamiatin, who is by profession an architect, is
considered by Gorky to be one of the coming Russian writers. A quaint little symbolic tale written
by him as a defence of free speech which he gave
me and which has never been translated into English before I reproduce here:

THURSDAY

There were two brothers living in a wood; the
senior and the junior. The senior was illiterate,
the junior, learned. About Easter they began to
argue between themselves. The senior said, "It's
Easter Sunday, time to eat Easter meals."

But the junior looked at the senior and replied,
"It's only Thursday."

The senior was furious and thought the junior
obstinate, stubborn. He fell upon him with an
axe, crying: "Will you not eat Easter meals? Say
you it is only Thursday?"

"It is only Thursday."

"Thursday? Thou damned one!" bellowed the
senior and hewed the junior down with the axe
and hid him under the seat. Then he heated the
oven, somehow ate Easter meals and sat under the
ikons, contented. Suddenly under the oven the
chirping of a cricket. Thursday—Thursday,

Thursday—Thursday, Thursday—Thursday. The senior was furious and crept under the oven.

There he searched for the cricket and came out all sooted, dreadful, black. But the cricket was caught, hewed down and the senior perspired, opened the windows and sat under the ikons contented. "Now it's all over," he said.

But outside below the windows, heaven knows whence, came sparrows, singing — Thursday, Thursday—Thursday.

More furious than ever was the senior. He went after the sparrows with his axe. Some flew away, some were hewed down. "Well, thank Heaven, it's finished—that damn word Thursday."

His axe was blunt from so much killing. He began to sharpen it and heard it jingle—Thursday—Thursday, Thursday. The senior threw down the axe and hid in the shrubs and there he lay until Easter.

On Easter Sunday the junior, naturally, rose from the dead. He crept out from under the seat and said to the senior: "Thou fool, to try to hew down a word. We are both right. Come kiss me, it's Easter."

While the Soviets declared a temporary suppression of the press, they never at any time tried to interfere with public speaking or with theatrical performances which ridiculed them or the revolution. I have often watched a crowd of rich bourgeoisie bullying sailor guards in front of the City Duma and marvelled at the patience of the sailors. Street talks were common. Red Guards would stand quietly listening to a speaker berate them without getting the least ruffled; they seemed often deeply interested in the arguments put up by their opponents. People do not shoot each other in Russia as a result of heated "discussions"; fist-fighting is practically unknown. Whenever there is fighting one can be sure that it is no personal thing but a mass action, a regular battle, no matter how small.

The Bolsheviki have been so long suppressed that when it falls their lot now to suppress other people they do it half-heartedly. This attitude was particularly beneficial to the prisoners in Peter and Paul Fortress. I went out to the prison one bitter day in January, because I had heard tales of the terrible hardships the prisoners had to undergo.

I was surprised and delighted to find that there were fires in all the cells, because in the government hotel where I lived we did not have enough fuel to heat the place and were literally freezing.

I walked along the corridor and found Bielinsky, the old Chief of Police under the Tsar, smiling with satisfaction. Even Sukomlinov, who sold out the army at the beginning of the war and who deserved death if any one ever did, was pleased with his treatment. For the first time since their imprisonment these men were permitted to walk in the courtyard and allowed to read the newspapers. All the prisoners were comfortable and had enough food. That was better than the rest of us on the "outside" could say.

We told the Bolshevik jailers and guards when we were leaving that we would like to take a room in the prison so we could keep warm, but they refused to joke about it. One of them said: "We know what it is like to be shut up for long days and nights. Nothing can make up for liberty."

It is interesting to note that the political prisoners liberated through the tolerance of the Bolsheviki now form their principal political opposition abroad.

CHAPTER XXIII

STREET FIGHTING

EVERY morning after the Bolshevik coup d'état I used to call at Smolny and at the City Duma. They both gave out news quite willingly. I had passes from both to go around the city and get into all the battles I wanted to. The Committee on Saving the Country and the Revolution sat in continual session and outdid any American advertising agency I ever came across. They used to tell us the wildest yarns. When I investigated I invariably found their statements untrue or at least ridiculously exaggerated. Once I went to Mayor Schroeder and complained. "At home," I said, "a politician wouldn't do that; he would really be afraid to tell a reporter a deliberate story. Now, the other night you told me that the prisoners in Peter and Paul were being massacred and I went way out there at two o'clock in the morning and found them sleeping peaceably in their beds."

He stroked his beard and looked serious, righteous almost. "Well," he said, "they (meaning the Bolsheviki) have all the force of arms on their side and we have, after all, only the moral force."

At Smolny they were frank enough, often thoroughly discouraged, never overrating their victories or underestimating their defeats. I think this remarkable way they had of facing the music was one of the greatest reasons for their success.

On the particular morning that I want to tell about, when I arrived at Smolny I found one of the officials very ill. I came back into town with a Bolshevik who is very close to Trotsky. We went straight to the Hotel Europe, where the American Red Cross had its headquarters, in search of a Red Cross doctor. As we walked through the lobby I was surprised to see one of Kerensky's aides standing in a corner with his arms folded and looking tragically funny. He had spent a lot of time in Babushka's quarters at the Winter Palace and I had known him quite well. He was, like all Russian officers of the old type, rather dandified and a little too immaculate and perfumed to please an American, but he was a Georgian and, like most of his race, so exceptionally handsome with his dark eyes and olive skin that you had to forgive him his overfastidiousness.

To-day, however, he was a changed man. He wore a coat too small and trousers too large and his waxed, pointed moustache was all frayed at the ends. He had on the most amazing tattered cap. I almost burst out laughing. It was so Russian for him to do it that way. Just because he was in disguise, in hiding, he would feel it necessary to wear a make-up that would point him out to every one as a conventional villain. It was with great difficulty that I stared right through him and passed on.

My Bolshevik friend and I climbed the wide stairs and walked along the corridor. When we were near the end the young Georgian caught up with us, he was all out of breath. "Mademoiselle," he exclaimed, taking both my hands, "did you not recognise me? I am in disguise!"

Russians can never keep secrets. It is one of the things I like best about them. Good, bad or indifferent their lives are an open book. But on this occasion I very much regretted this national lack of repression. In vain I tried to silence him by winks and cold stares. He couldn't imagine what was wrong with me. He was lonesome and glad to see a friend and that is all he thought about. He blurted out all sorts of startling information. "Kerensky will be here by to-morrow with eighty thousand Cossacks. We will take all the Bolshevik leaders and string them up along the streets!"

"O please don't talk about it," I said, feeling awfully responsible for the serious trouble he was getting himself into. But he misunderstood me entirely and said soothingly: "Now don't you worry, no one is going to hurt you."

We did not escape from him until he had unburdened himself of every scrap of information and misinformation he possessed.   It never occurred to him to enquire the politics of my companion.

"What are you going to do?" I asked my friend from Smolny when we were out on the street again.

"Have him arrested," he answered shortly.   We entered into a long argument.   I maintained that he was of no importance and ought to be treated like the aristocrats who were living in peace all over the city.   There is the Grand Duke Constantine's family, for example, who live in the Marble Palace. They occupy the top floor while all the rest of the building is used by the Bureau of Labour. . . .

We were not able to finish the argument because as we turned the corner of Gogol street and St. Isaacs Square sniping began from roof tops.   A man walking in front of the German Embassy suddenly dropped down dead, shot by the bullet of an unknown enemy.   Cronstadt sailors, on guard at the Astoria Hotel, come rushing down the street to locate the offenders, shouting *"Provocatsia!"* People were always being killed in those first days by snipers just to start riots.   The working people did not want riots and it was easy enough to place the blame.

We could hear firing going on about a block away.   The Junkers had taken the telephone exchange on the Morskaya and the Bolsheviki had surrounded them.   Bullets began to fly too generally for comfort.   We hid in a courtyard behind

the Angleterre Hotel and through the chinks in
the fence we watched the ridiculous, padded Russian cabmen—*isvoschicks*—who usually amble
along like snails, whipping up their horses and rapidly clearing the square.

As soon as it became quieter we started back to
Gogol street. At the corner we saw an armoured
car coming at full speed. We did not have time to
seek shelter. We found ourselves crammed against
a closed archway that had great iron doors securely
locked. We hoped that the car would go on, but
directly in front of us it stopped with a jerk as if
something had gone wrong with the machinery. It's
destination was quite evidently the telephone exchange. We had no way of knowing which side it
was on until it began to spout fire, shooting up the
street and occasionally right into our midst. Then
we knew that it belonged to the Junkers. There
were twenty in our crowd and about six were Cronstadt sailors.

The first victim was a working man. His right
leg was shattered and he sank down without a
sound, gradually turning paler and losing consciousness as a pool of blood widened around him.
Not one of us dared to move. A man in an expensive fur coat kept repeating monotonously:
"I'm sick of this revolution!"

All that happened in the next few minutes is not
exactly clear—we were all so excited. One thing
that I remember, which struck me even then, was

that no one in our crowd screamed, although seven were killed. I remember also the two little street boys. One whimpered pitifully when he was shot, the other died instantly, dropping at our feet an inanimate bundle of rags, his pinched little face covered with his own blood. I remember the old peasant woman who kept crossing herself and whispering prayers. . . .

The hopelessness of our position was just beginning to sink in on me when the sailors with a great shout ran straight into the fire. They succeeded in reaching the car and thrust their bayonets inside again and again. The sharp cries of the victims rose above the shouting, and then suddenly everything was sickeningly quiet. They dragged three dead men out of the armoured car and they lay face up on the cobbles, unrecognisable and stuck all over with bayonet wounds.

Only the chauffeur escaped. He begged for mercy and my companion from Smolny said to the sailors: "For God's sake let him go—let's not kill any more of them than we have to." It was a most characteristic remark. Russians hate violence and they hate to kill. At a time like that Anglo-Saxons or almost any other race would have been insane with rage at the death of their seven comrades. But the Russians let the chauffeur go. . . .

We came back to the argument about Kerensky's aide as we strolled up the Nevsky. "I will tell you what I will do," said he, "I'll give him three days to get out—if he isn't out then he will have to go to prison!" I don't think he ever thought of the aide again. And in three days Kerensky's troops had been defeated and Kerensky himself was in disguise.

One of the most amusing things I heard about disguises was a story concerning Avksentieff, who was one time extremely influential with the peasants until he voted for coalition at the Democratic Congress. By that vote he lost not only his position and his popularity, but his long silky whiskers of which he was particularly proud. Madame Lebedev, Prince Kropotkin's daughter, sheared them off for him when she helped him out of Petrograd.

In Moscow and some of the small towns much more bitter street fighting occurred than in Petrograd. The most bloody battle of the week was for the possession of the Vladimir Officers' School. The officers who were defending the place finally put up a white flag, whereupon the Red Guards came out of their barricades and walked across the open street. Midway the officers opened fire and a number of the revolutionists were killed. In the wild confusion that followed the people stormed the school, took it and stuck some of the officers up on their bayonets. I have always imagined that the whole unfortunate affair occurred because of lack of co-ordination on the part of the Junkers. It seems impossible that they would have been so stupid as to have deliberately fired after surrendering, knowing they were greatly out-numbered, although a similar affair occurred in Moscow. The officers seemed incapable of realising that they were no longer in power.

CHAPTER XXIV

MEN OF HONOUR

ON the morning of January 9th I sat at breakfast in the grand dining room of the Astoria Hotel. Tired soldiers slouched in and out looking strangely out of place in a magnificent setting that was built as a background for gay ladies and flashing officers. There had been neither lights nor water for two days and the Tartar waiter had just informed us that the bread had run out, but we could still have *chi*—tea. A soldier at the next table offered me part of a can of fish and another leaned over and said: "Well, Comrade, they are here." He was speaking of the German and Austrian delegates. For a long time we had been expecting them—ever since the negotiations had begun at Brest-Litovsk.

As Americans we were not permitted to get interviews, but there was no law against "looking" at one's enemy. As soon as we could we located them and after that all the correspondents spent a good deal of time watching the delegates stow away their rabchick. Rabchick is a little Russian wild bird, that and cabbage were virtually all we had to eat in those days. There were high officers with their aides and stenographers—altogether numbering about forty. They sat at long tables chattering volubly. Above the tables were the same old signs: "Don't speak German!"

There were two delegations—one stopped at the Hotel Bristol on the Moika and was headed by Rear-Admiral Count Kaiserling and Count von Mirbach who has since been assassinated in Moscow. His committee was known as the Naval Delegation and their mission was to discuss means of stopping the naval war in accordance with the armistice treaty. The second delegation was headed by Count Berchtold, German Red Cross representative, and met to consider the exchange of war prisoners. They established themselves at the Grand and the Angleterre. British and French officers were stopping at both these places, which was obviously embarrassing. Almost all the delegates had in some way been connected with the German and Austrian embassies before the war, and several had had property in Russia and two were big German merchants.

It was the business of Dr. Zalkind, Trotsky's assistant, to call at their hotels to see if they had secured enough rooms.

At exactly the right number of hours and wearing the proper attire for such occasions, von Mirbach returned Zalkind's visit at the Foreign Office as if it had been an official call. The *svetzar* brought in the card. Zalkind was busy, but he pushed back the papers on his desk, got up and walked into the hallway.

"Hello!" he said, "what are you doing here?"

The count was abashed. "Why, I am just returning your call," he said stiffly.

Zalkind was amused. "Excuse me, Count," he said, "we are revolutionists and we don't recognise ceremony. You might have saved yourself the trouble if you had remembered that you are in New Russia." He thought a minute. "But you can come in," he added, "and have a glass of tea."

Von Mirbach did not accept the invitation. He looked down at Zalkind's rough clothes, his rumpled grey hair and his inspired face. Very awkwardly he got himself out of the alien atmosphere of the Foreign Office.

Trotsky ordered the Red Guard to mount guard over the hotels where the delegates were staying. Almost immediately a clamour went up. Count Kaiserling and all the rest of them maintained that they were "men of honour" and that such suspicion on the part of the Bolsheviki was ridiculous and an insult. So the guards were withdrawn, but the confidence of the Bolsheviki in the word of the German delegates was not strong enough to prevent them from retaining the Secret Service.

A week passed.

In the Hotel Europe wild speculation was going on. Rich Russian business men were falling over each other to get in touch with the delegates. And the Germans were evidently in a frenzy to enter into big contracts with them. The Bolsheviki took note of all this. From every part of Russia hidden supplies suddenly came to light. As far East as Siberia cars were mysteriously loaded with rubber and wheat. As far South as the Caucasus food was packed ready for shipping. And these were the same "upper classes" who had shut their ears and their hearts to the pitiful appeals of the starving and desperate soldiers. In Finland the bourgeoisie were more active than usual. . . .

I remember a large and pompous German speculator, a member of the delegation, who appeared at this time. He used to stroll up and down the crowded and battered Nevsky Prospect about eleven o'clock every morning. He wore a high silk hat, and he did not deign to glance at the miserable and curious population. He was so altogether smug that I used to wish his ears would freeze or some other misfortune would befall him, but nothing ever happened. He was immune to everything Russian —even the weather.

Taking it all in all, there is little difference between speculators in one country or another. And in every country they wax fat in wartime—like ghouls.

One day when all this had gone far enough, the Bolsheviki put back the guard—*doubled!* The men of honour understood and said not a word. Many persons connected with the affair were arrested.

But the poor people of Russia, used for centuries to being sold out by the bourgeoisie, when they learned the truth through the soldiers' papers, were not even surprised.

Kaiserling, during his visit in Petrograd, gave an interview to a reporter on the *Dien*. In answer to the query of whether or not he thought Bolshevism would cross the frontier into Germany, he said ironically: "If Bolshevism is a danger to us, why is it not a danger for France or for England?"

The Russian ruffled him considerably by his next remark. "Yes, but you cannot deny that Germany is our nearest neighbour, so don't you think that the Russian Revolution will naturally have more influence on the masses in Germany than in distant countries? And you will not deny that there has been serious mutiny in the German fleet."

Kaiserling hedged. "There were troubles on certain boats," he confessed, "but they were quickly suppressed and the guilty were properly punished. In general your insinuations are vain. At home all goes better and better. We have full constitutional liberty. And in this regard treacherous England herself is the most abominable state in the universe. Even the United States can envy us."

Reporter—Have you had the pleasure of seeing Trotsky, chief of our external affairs?

Kaiserling—No, I have not had this pleasure. I have tried on five occasions to shake his hand cordially, but up to the present time he has been too busy to see me.

Most of the time the Count answered questions about his government with phrases like this: "We are entirely tranquil." "Russian anarchy cannot affect Germany." He asked the reporter what the demonstration that the Bolsheviki were arranging for the following day was meant to signify.

The demonstration he spoke of was held on January 21. It was one of the largest demonstrations that has taken place since the first revolution. About a quarter of a million people took part in it, and it lasted all day. There were Red Guards, Cronstadt sailors, women and children—all working people. We had heard that it was a peace demonstration and wondered if it could be possible that they expected a decent peace to be signed at Brest. However, it turned out to be nothing of the sort. *Everybody in the parade was armed!* It was a solemn and menacing procession and yet most of the banners bore the one word, "Peace."

I am sure the Germans never understood what the Russians meant by that great parade. They felt only that they were somehow insulted, and that was all. But there was a much deeper significance. The people who marched through the snow-covered streets knew that they *had* to have peace—that they were, for the hour, at the end of things. At the same time it was a forced peace which left every man and woman and child with future wars to fight; it was an armed peace.   And this was only their peculiar Russian way of expressing what they felt.   Before every marcher was a vision of a day when the German militarists who now stood gloating over them should no longer hold in terror a tired and aching world.   Almost every demonstration in Russia has a certain symbolic meaning.

CHAPTER XXV

GERMAN PROPAGANDA

GERMAN propaganda is by no means as blatant and unfinished a thing as we generally believe. Stories of how German agents bought up whole regiments of Russian soldiers are ridiculously untrue. Along the Russian front it was dangerous even to give away cigarettes. An American correspondent, who was at the front in November, felt so sorry for the soldiers that he went back to the nearest town behind the lines and bought a lot of cigarettes. When he returned to the trenches he began to distribute them rather freely. He was almost mobbed. When his papers were examined and he had explained, they finally let him go. But after that he found it so unpleasant that he decided to return to Petrograd. The rumour that he was a German agent spread and when he was waiting for his train at the little railway station the next day he was again surrounded by soldiers and threatened. . . . Those of us who tried to find out how the Germans managed their propaganda found their methods very subtle and hard to trace. They never blundered to the extent of trying to openly buy the common soldiers—they purchased the services of those who could directly or indirectly influence them.

When they found they could not buy the revolutionary leaders they did their best to besmirch them. In Russia one can purchase fake evidence by the pound to prove that Lenine and Trotsky are German agents. All this evidence was absolutely disproved by the Provisional Government while it held these men for trial. And yet this German propaganda has been more or less successful. It was not very long ago that one of our officials came rushing home with a trunkful and but for the efforts of a few sane representatives, the Russian situation would have been more complicated than it is.

The German Bureau of Propaganda, which centres in Berlin, has on its staff members of every profession who are expert in their various lines. Their special aim is to study the psychology of the people they wish to reach. For example, if they wish to do propaganda in Russia they secure the services of some one who knows the Russian mind and who has probably lived in Russia a long time and is located in Berlin. The ground is carefully gone over and when the bureau decides what to do they instruct in great detail their agents with whom they are in touch. These agents have been sent to live in different localities and are not generally suspected.

The most illuminating example that I came across extended over a long period and as it unravelled I began to understand many other things. In Stockholm, on the way over, I met a young woman who said that she was an American correspondent.   She was frankly pro-German.

A number of us, all reporters, were lunching at the Grand and after luncheon she walked with me towards my hotel.   I said that I was looking for a fur coat and she said without any hesitation at all: "Why, don't get it here—everything is so expensive, I'll get it for you in Germany."

I stopped, thinking for a minute that I had misunderstood.   But the young woman only laughed. "I know what you are going to say," she continued, "you are going to say that it is trafficking with the enemy, but that is very narrow-minded of you."

By this time we had reached my destination.   I watched her swinging down the street; she had blonde hair and a ruddy skin and everything about her seemed more German than American.   Remembering some of her remarks at luncheon about how fine the Prussian officers were, I hoped that I was correct in my surmise.

I never saw her again and this story is not altogether to do with her, but she is an important link. Five months later she was ordered arrested by Allied authorities and she fled into Germany where she still remains.   Her latest activity was to publish a book called "Mein Lieber Barbars."

In Petrograd there was only one paper published in English.   The editor was a weak-kneed, vacillating little person with no opinions of his own and he was dominated by a particularly despicable little character who claimed to be a Russian when he was in America and an American when he was in Russia. In both places he managed to escape military service.

Certain articles written by him caused much hard feeling in Russia against America. He attacked Trotsky and the Bolsheviki just after they came into power. It is easy to imagine how we might have felt if a foreign paper, published in this country, had begun to attack President Lincoln during the Civil War, every day filling its pages with false reports about the "barbaric" actions of the North.

The Bolsheviki were puzzled as to just what to do. The owners kept in the background and paid little attention to the policy. Several times the English and the American correspondents spoke of making a formal protest against the paper, but somehow no action was ever taken. Often in Smolny excited Russians would say to us accusingly: "So this is how the American papers lie about the revolutionists!" And we would explain, with vehemence, that the paper was not an American publication.

A very cleverly worded story about the six days' fighting in Moscow when the Bolsheviki overcame the Junkers, began in this way: "An American returning from Moscow reports that German officers had charge of the Bolshevik guns."

The wicked part of that article was not so much that the whole story was a lie, but that it was put in just that way—*an American says* . . .

The man who wrote it told a Russian who worked in the same office not to let certain Americans know that he was sending out news to the young lady who said she could get me a fur coat in Germany. And the Russian, being as curious as a child, hastened to tell us because he couldn't imagine what the mystery was about and because no Russian can keep a secret.

I went in to see this man one day just after he had printed an article about a German officer standing on the Nikolaisky Voksaal (station) and haranguing a crowd of Russians for an hour, calling them dogs, etc. I asked him why he printed that story which he knew to be untrue and he claimed to have seen the officer. He said there were many Germans in Smolny. I answered that I went there almost daily and had never encountered any. "Well," he said slyly, "I have been forbidden to enter Smolny, but as long as you go there freely, why don't you bring me the news? You can name your price and if you don't want to do it, get some one who can."

And this was not all. He made a deliberate effort to get the confidence of the Allied Ambassadors and for a time he succeeded with one of them.

The latest disclosures of German intrigue in the

United States directly connect these characters in my story with the *Evening Mail* fund.

Once when there was a rumour that the Germans would be in Petrograd within a few days—this was just after the fall of Riga—the same man confided to an American girl that she need not worry. All she would have to do, he said, was to mention the name of the woman in Stockholm to the German officers and she would be treated with great respect.

Another sheet which was violently anti-Bolshevik was *l'Entente,* a paper formerly published in Roumania and later transferred to Petrograd. Finally the Bolsheviki shut it up and the editor, an unscrupulous little man, went to see Dr. Zalkind, Assistant Minister of Foreign Affairs, to make "an arrangement." He explained to Zalkind that if he would give him permission to open his paper again he would make it pro-Bolshevik. Zalkind smiled and the editor decided that he had won his point. In Russia there is a new law that if a paper is closed down it cannot appear again under the same name. And the wily editor, remembering, remarked to Zalkind as he rose to depart: "Now the only thing left to settle is the name . . . Could you suggest one?"

Zalkind thought a moment and replied gravely: "Yes . . . I should call such a paper . . . *'The Prostitute.'* "

The best and only authentic information from all parts of Russia was gathered by the French government. Every day a bulletin of multigraphed copies was issued and only a few rubles a month was charged for the service. It contained unprejudiced news, without comment, and also translations of leading editorials from *all* the Russian papers. An American newspaper pursuing such a neutral policy could not help but be of real benefit.

The German propagandists in Russia have made a tremendous effort to hurt President Wilson in the eyes of the working people. They have held up the Mooney trial as "an example of our supposed democracy." They have made use of our lynching cases and every suppressive measure against our radicals. It is too bad that we continue to have these examples for them to point to because there is no argument to refute them. We ourselves are at a loss. . . .

Along the front, on the German side, a huge poster used to be displayed, showing President Wilson pushing the Russian soldiers into battle and holding his own away from the danger.

German propagandists would make little headway if all our diplomats were as sensitive to situations as Colonel Raymond Robbins, head of the American Red Cross Mission. He never spared himself any difficult task to further friendship between Russia and America. He never assumed an antagonistic attitude toward any group of Russian people. He supported the Provisional Government; he supported the Soviets. No matter how fast the changes came or how sweeping they happened to be, he immediately made himself familiar with them. I think every correspondent will agree with me that, according to their best observation, Colonel Robbins did more to offset unfavourable impressions, was more valuable and actually accomplished more than any other man or group of men sent to Russia by the United States Government.

When Colonel Robbins left Russia he was given a special train through Siberia and accorded every honour from the Soviet government. Nothing proves better, to my mind, the common ground for friendship than this confidence of the Russian masses in Colonel Robbins. Robbins has never pretended to be a Socialist nor has he upheld the banners of the conservatives; he has merely made an honest effort to be impartial.

Russia is the greatest undeveloped land in the world; it is infinitely rich in raw materials. Germany realises that. After the war there must be keen competition for Russian trade. And this is where German propaganda must essentially fail. *She has tried to take by force what she might have had by extending friendship.* Of course it was almost impossible for her to extend friendship because of the incompatibility of the two governments. There is only one course left for her to pursue. The Russians will never forget the forced and unjust "peace" which followed the Brest-Litovsk negotiations. So she must attempt by every means possible to keep Russia and other nations, *especially the United States,* on unfriendly terms and *she must overthrow the Soviet government or even a more moderate government.* She must establish a government more like her own. Of course, if we are wise and foreseeing enough, we will not fall into Germany's trap. We will offer aid to Russia and assume toward her a large tolerance and we will officially recognise *whatever government* there is—without regard to its political views or our own prejudices in the matter.

CHAPTER XXVI

RUSSIAN CHILDREN

A MERICA has shown great sympathy for the children of Belgium, of Serbia, of Poland, of all the little warring countries swept by the fire of war. As a nation we have accomplished splendid relief work for which we will never be forgotten. But in our eagerness to aid the small nations we have almost overlooked great Russia. While the wildest exaggerations fill our daily papers, Russia herself does not consciously advertise her sufferings as other nations do. We have little correct information as to just how pitiful conditions are in that vast land of a hundred and eighty million, so we haven't faced the terrible fact that *more children have died in Russia since the war than in all the little countries together*.

Ever since the beginning, nearly four years ago, conditions have been unbearable for the children. Transportation, never very efficient, was almost completely upset as soon as mobilisation began and it was never reorganised. Children in the cities have been without proper nourishment for four years because milk and other necessities have not been brought in from the rural districts. At first, the country children were not greatly affected, but as the war went on and disorganisation spread, King Hunger claimed them all. I used to wonder last year how any of them survived. I once asked a doctor who has had experience in caring for children in six warring countries and he said that the only explanation he could offer was that Russian children have more resistance than other children. "I was forced to give them food in my hospital," he said, "that American babies would have died on in a few days. . . ."

If it is true that Russian children are so strong it only makes the statistics regarding their mortality more tragic. On the retreats in Galicia, out of Volhynia, Riga, and other places, they died at the rate of *800 out of every 1000*. *In the charitable institutions,* overcrowded, disease ridden, unsanitary, lacking almost every medical necessity, *only 15 per cent. survived.*

Just to write this down, or to speak of it cannot give a mental picture to any one who has not actually seen such a sweeping scourge of the little people. It begins to sink into you after you have lived in Russia for some time and you begin to wonder where the children have gone. I went along always looking for the happy youngsters to whom the bright toys in the shop windows, now dust-covered, should belong. I came to realise with horror that everybody in Russia is grown up. Those young in years, whom we still called children, had old and sad faces, large, hungry eyes burned forth from pale countenances, wretched, worn-out shoes, sagging, ragged little garments accentuated their so apparent misery.

In Petrograd last winter, Colonel Raymond Robbins, of the American Red Cross, made an attempt to supply the babies of Petrograd with canned milk, but all sorts of delays in shipping occurred, policies toward Russia changed, so that when I left late in January the milk had not yet arrived. To be sure, speculators somehow managed to smuggle in small consignments and 10c cans of popular American brands could be bought at the exorbitant rate of 16½ rubles. I wish I could efface from my memory the old peasant women and the little ragamuffins who stood in the snow outside the grocery windows gazing wistfully at the little red and white cans.*

On the retreats confusion and terror swept along with the refugees. Last autumn when they were fleeing down the muddy roads before the advancing Germans, parents had no time to stop to bury their dead children. Mothers fell exhausted and died with live babies in their arms. Long cherished bits of household treasures, dragged along with the hope of making another home somewhere, were dropped all along the weary miles; here a chest,

* Col. Robbins in February and March distributed several hundred thousand cans of milk to Petrograd babies.

there an old hand-wrought kettle, a brass samovar. . . . Hatless, coatless, hungry, often bare-
footed and knee-deep in slush the population
pushed doggedly along for days.

Even on the more organised retreats where Red
Cross doctors had charge, sick children had to be
left behind in military hospitals, especially was this
true if the children had contagious diseases like
scarlet fever. They were hastily placed in separate
wards and tags were tied to their clothing, and on
the door was pasted a notice addressed to the Germans, giving brief information about the ailment
of the child, who its parents were, where they came
from, and their destination. There was a desperate
hope that the parent and child would one day find
each other, but in most cases the hope was vain.

A beautiful camaraderie between the children on
these marches existed. The older ones often carried the younger and as they tramped along they
sang folk songs, intermingled with all the new revolutionary tunes. Their lovely little high sopranos,
sifting through the cold heavy dampness of the
dreary Russian autumn and their huddled little figures through the mist gave them the appearance of
a phantom army of all the children who have died
in this war for the sins of a few diplomats sitting
around a gilded table, plotting conquest and spill-
ing the world's blood.

The children showed remarkable courage, standing all sorts of hardships without whimpering. This

was especially true of the children who were sent
ahead of the parents in order that, even if the parents perished, the children at least might be saved.
In the strangeness and turmoil of the new life, individuals asserted themselves. One little boy or
girl, often by no means the oldest, might lead a band
of twenty or thirty. He would make himself a self-
appointed chief, sometimes displaying rank favour-
itism.

Life was not all serious in these sad little armies.
The children found time to play jokes on the doctors, to tease the nurses and to mimic the revolutionary leaders. They formed committees and issued proclamations of defiance, pretending to refuse orders from superiors. This aping of the new
life was true in the schools of Petrograd. Little
boys laboriously wrote out long documents and
pasted them on the walls, "just like Lenine and
Trotsky." One of the teachers told me an amusing
tale about a committee of youngsters who came to
her with the portentous information that thereafter
the students in the school would receive no orders
"unless countersigned by the committee," the oldest member of the committee being twelve years
old.

The only child I ever knew who seemed to enjoy
the hazards of war was an amazingly beautiful boy
by the name of Vanya, son of a well-to-do peasant
from the province of Volhynia. He was lost at one
of the stations where he had gotten out to get water

for tea. In all the railway stations there are huge tankards of boiling water for those who are travelling and the peasants always carry with them big brass kettles for brewing tea, which they drink almost every hour of the day.

Vanya had persuaded his parents to let him get the water "just once" after the manner of little boys. Then it seems that he became interested in a large friendly dog and forgot his mission. The train went off and the parents did not discover that he was missing until they were many miles away; and refugees cannot turn back. For hours Vanya stood waiting for the train to return. Toward dusk he was found by a company of Cossacks going toward the front.

His adventures after that were so remarkable that he became a legendary character and was reported to have a charmed life. For weeks he rode at the head of the Cossack regiment on a fiery charger. He became the idol of the camp and the Cossacks loaded him down with all sorts of presents looted along the way. He wore these round his neck in loops like a little savage. Cossacks are gentle with but two living things—children and horses.

Vanya had a genius for being lost. He was lost by the Cossacks and wandered aimlessly through a lonely wood eating wild berries and sleeping under the stars. He was found by a woodcutter and his wife and adopted by them and loved as a son. But they also, in their turn, had to flee from the Germans, and after a long journey reached Petrograd.

Here Vanya was lost again and found by an American and brought to the American Refuge Home, which was established at the beginning of the war by subscriptions raised among the members of the American legation and added to by friends in America. It never grew to much importance, but those who kept up an interest were able to care for about forty children.

The story of how Vanya was at last found by his parents after he had wandered all over Russia for a year and a half is one of the exceptional happy endings to the thousands of sad tales of scattered and broken lives of the people from the invaded districts.

To be of assistance in bringing together lost families was the principal business of the Grand Duchess Tatiana Committee which posted semiweekly lists of the refugees in the various camps. It was by this means that Vanya's father read Vanya's name on one of the lists. He had walked twenty *versts* twice a week to the office of the Committee to procure the lists for over a year. . . .

Famine has threatened Russia for months and now it seems inevitable. There is little or no seed for the next planting, lack of horses and farming implements, no means of transportation, while the grain stores in the Ukraine are being seized by the Germans or burned by the peasants to keep them from the enemy's hands; in Siberia the supplies are held up for one reason or another. For so long we have believed every odious, unsympathetic tale that comes out of Russia, tales meant purposely to poison our minds and make us hostile. In other words, we have believed just exactly what the Germans have wanted us to believe. But whatever vast differences of opinion we may hold with the majority of the Russian people, children are the same to us all the world over. Eventually we will have to aid Russian children as generously as children of other countries.

CHAPTER XXVII

THE DECLINE OF THE CHURCH

RUSSIA, in my imagination, had always been "holy" Russia, and it was surprising to go there and find it so apparently unholy. The shrines along the streets loomed blackly, forgotten and unlit. The churches for the most part were silent and deserted. I had expected to see vast religious changes with the revolution, but what I found was so sweeping and so sudden. A year before scarcely any one passed a church without crossing himself —the soldiers, the cabmen. Now only occasionally one of the crowd makes his gesture of respect absent mindedly, like an old courtier bowing to a dead king.

Happily no matter what changes may come the churches will remain a striking part of the Russian landscape. I used to think when I looked out of my window in Moscow that it could scarcely matter whether or not one ever went inside, because it was impossible not to get spiritual inspiration by merely looking at the beautiful exteriors. Moscow has the most exquisite skylines, the flat-topped colourful Russian dwellings broken up by the tall golden spires, the green and blue domes with the

slender crosses.   Moscow is full of churches and so
is all Russia.   In the Caucasus the traveller runs
suddenly across a jewel of a little church, of ivory
and blue, nestled in the dark evergreens. . . .

And the bells are beyond description.   Sometimes
a low sweet chime comes to you from a great distance, a faint silver tinkle; sometimes the bells of
all the world seem to be ringing at once in a great
barbaric symphony.

Russians are deeply religious, like the Irish or the
Italians, and they will always be religious.   But
the church to-day in their minds is all knit with the
Tsar and the old régime and is naturally absolutely
discredited.   Once the Little Father was divine, now
he is only a poor exile with all his weaknesses ex-
posed and they are disillusioned.   Autocracy was
an integral part of the old religion.   When the Russian church produced such monsters as Rasputin,
Iliodor and Bishop Pitirim it had reached the
height of its corruption and was rotten to the core.
And like the monarchy, it crumpled and disappeared without a struggle at the first firm blow;
it was but a shell.   And the masses, a simple, mys-
tical people, turned the channel of their ardour into
revolutionary enthusiasm, into the idea of world
freedom and internationalism.

The intelligentsia have always been largely athe-
istic.   This swerving away from the church now
is all by the peasants.   Yet they do not harbour a
violent resentment.   I bought old ikons in the

markets and put them up around my room. Almost every one who came in remarked about my having them there. If they were intelligentsia they laughed at my "piety." If they were working people they were puzzled and displeased. I explained that they were very beautiful—interesting from a point of art. "They cannot be beautiful to us," they would exclaim, "blind faith in them has caused us too much sorrow." In the old days a man carried an ikon when he went forth to kill a man as well as when he went to bless one.

I talked to Y. M. C. A. men who had spent many months in all parts of Russia. They all told me the same thing. The old Orthodox Greek Church is dead. In their opinion this was greatly due to the fact that it offered so little and demanded so much. As Dillon has recently remarked: "It (the church) was a mere museum of liturgical antiquities. No life-giving ever animated that rigid body, for Byzance was powerless to give what it did not possess." The Y. M. C. A. representatives are not hopeless over the situation. They believe that it is only a matter of time before a more satisfactory, more human institution is built in its place.

An incident which I witnessed in Petrograd in December illustrates an amusing new resentment among the people for the superior feeling of the priests. I was riding on a street car one morning when a priest climbed aboard. He refused to pay his fare, saying he was a man of God and therefore exempt. Immediately the passengers became excited. They were mostly peasants and they began to argue hotly. A man of God, they claimed, was no different from any other man—all were equal since the revolution. But the priest was stubborn and not until the crowd threatened to take him to the Revolutionary Tribunal did he consent to pay, grumbling.

Priests were employed at the funerals after the February revolution, but the rift between the church and the people widened quickly. On the greatest occasions like the famous Red Burial there were no priests and no ceremony. I shall never forget the menacing and hostile glances we received when we went through the Kremlin the day after the funeral. The Red Guards took us through so we could make a correct report of the damages. The priests were so enraged over the Junker defeat that they would not even speak—but they were powerless. I had a feeling that if they had the power instead of the masses there would have been terrible revenge and bloodshed.

There are many noticeable evidences of paganism in the Russian church. It has been the study of the church to combat this by purifying what they could not uproot by turning to account any similarity of names or of symbols. It explains the high place of honour given St. George and St. Dmitrie, the slayers of dragons, and the festival song in honour of St. John which runs: "John and Mary bathed on the hill—while John bathed the earth shook—while Mary bathed the earth germinated." The sacred trees and the mysterious wells have all been consecrated to the saints and purified with holy rites.

One of these pagan customs was the annual blessing of the Neva. In January of this year the Neva went unblessed. I saw the whole dismal performance.

There were half a dozen priests and about twenty old peasants. They gathered in St. Isaacs Cathedral, and after a good deal of singing and burning of incense, they emerged from the great doors and down the broad steps. A small blizzard had just come up. The streets were knee-deep in snow and as we walked we kept running into drifts. After proceeding about three blocks the priests stopped, sprinkled holy water and waved the incense burners, then they trod in a circle, looked at their scanty following, heaved great disappointed sighs and began to retreat toward the church. The peasants, without a word, dwindled away.

In Petrograd there was an entire lack of interest in the affair. I tried vainly to get several Russian friends to go with me to see the ceremony, but they only laughed and went on with their interminable discussions.

Russian priests never fit my idea of conventional priests at all. I saw two laughing merrily once while some old peasants were bowing their heads to the stone floor during mass. They often had mean, vicious faces, were extremely dissipated and commanded no respect from their flocks. One old priest who spent much time at the front, adored to tell the most frankly Rabelaisian stories. One of the peculiar things I found about these few remaining priests at the front was that the soldiers commanded them to pray for the horses and the deserters as well as themselves. This supervision of prayers was always a custom in Russia. Drunken priests were kicked awake and made to pray for a dying man or perform a marriage ceremony. What strange intermediaries to God!

The priests were forced to marry according to the law of the church, but the monks were celibate.

None of them seemed to feel that cleanliness was next to godliness, many of them did not wash at all. The village priests, always desperately poor, were a repulsive sight as they went along mumbling into their matted beards, their long dirty garments dragging on the sidewalk and half a dozen ragged children clinging to their arms. The one universal note was that neither the priests nor the monks liked to work. The great rich estates of the church were confiscated by the Bolsheviki and turned over to the peasants. The monks were invited to remain if they would promise to do their share of labour. The majority of them indignantly refused. Some of the younger ones, however, left the church and went into all sorts of service under the new government.

Madame Kollontay, Minister of Welfare, told me she had a number in her department. And some I know were teachers. What became of the rank and file no one seems to know. Of course, a few are still tending to the tag ends of their flocks.

No one, even the most devout, can feel sorry because of the sudden fall of the Russian church. Whatever is built in its place must be better and more solid and more satisfying even if it will not be so picturesque and semi-pagan.

CHAPTER XXVIII

ODDS AND ENDS OF REVOLUTION

THERE were many little incidents I came across in Russia that while of themselves are of no particular importance, yet gathered together may give the reader more atmosphere than a deliberate attempt at a picture. Now that I am home again and must depend for information largely on the reports sent out by Berlin or Vienna and meant to prejudice us against Russia, or by those of my colleagues who make it a business to write sensational stories, it seems but fair that I should tell of my own experiences and those of my friends in this supposed violent Russia. It is a great pity that all our correspondents are not as well balanced and as intelligent as Mr. Arthur Ransome,* whose despatches appear in the London *Daily News,* New York *Times,* and the *New Republic.* Mr. Ransome is an Englishman who has lived in Russia for a number of years and knows his ground well, he writes as an observer and not for or against any party in power, and that seems to me the only reasonable conduct for a reporter. No more clear-

* Mr. Ransome is also known as a novelist, a translator of Remy de Gourmont, and a teller of Russian fairy stories.

headed comment on the political situation in Russia has been publicly made than that which appeared in his "Letter to the American People" in which he said, "Remember any non-Soviet government in Russia would be welcomed by Germany and, reciprocally, *could not but regard Germany as its protector. Remember that the revolutionary movement in Eastern Europe, no less than in the American and British navies, is an integral part of the Allied blockade of the Central Empires."* If one goes to Russia and finds that the Soviet government is the expression of the people, it is quite necessary to say so, no matter what one may feel personally concerning the Soviet government.

If one expects to find nothing but bloodshed and one finds that there is much else, that one can go about in a fur coat without the least hindrance, that theatres, the ballet, movies and other more or less frivolous institutions still flourish, it may subdue the tone of one's tale, but it is highly necessary to note the fact. It is silly to defend the revolution by claiming there has been *no* bloodshed and it is just as silly to insist that the streets are running blood. We must use logic in deciding the truth of widely varying statements. There is, for example, that careful, scientific observer, Professor Albert Ross, who travelled 20,000 miles in Russia and "never saw a blow struck" and "instead of agitation and tumult, found habit still the lord of life" in comparison to a prejudiced reporter like

Herman Bernstein who somehow managed to see everywhere the wildest confusion, murders and robberies in broad daylight, cars falling off the tracks, the dead unburied and so on *ad infinitum*. No one can predict what will happen before the problem of a new government is settled in Russia, but up to the present moment the actions of the mass, so long mistreated and suppressed, and now suddenly given liberty has been surprisingly gentle.

If all the things that are supposed to be done are really done, I think *some* of them would have happened to me. I am a woman, not noticeably old, and I often travelled alone in Russia. I did not have one unpleasant, ugly experience. I was followed by spies, I was in battles, but in the first instance I was treading on dangerous ground and in the second instance it was because I chose to be in the centre of action. A few days ago I read with some amazement about a brave reporter who travelled all the way from Petrograd to Moscow and back to Petrograd again. It was the first time that I realised it *was* a brave thing. I did it many times, when the train was packed with hungry soldiers. Once I tried to divide my sandwiches with one. He had been standing up in the aisle all night and looked weary and miserable. He refused the food. "Eat it yourself, little comrade," he said, "it will be many hours before we reach the end of the journey."

A San Francisco newspaper woman, who was in Russia when I was there and who travelled home with me, often remarked with indignation on the exaggerations of conditions in Russia. She tells an amusing tale about an encounter she had with a Cossack shortly after her arrival at the Astoria Hotel in Petrograd. She had been filled with tales of the brutality of Cossacks and so she was quite naturally alarmed one evening to have a tall, handsome Cossack rap sharply on her door. When she opened it, he stepped into the room, closed the door, made a bow and took from his pocket a green sash. Miss B—— recognised it as her own. She realised at once that she must have dropped the sash going or coming from dinner. She wanted to thank the Cossack, but she did not speak Russian and she did not speak German. It occurred to her that many Russians speak French. She had a smattering of French. *"Merci—pour—cette,"* she murmured, taking the sash and pointing to her waist. The Cossack came closer, touched her dress and smiled. "Ah," he remarked in perfect English. "I understand, you do not wear corset." Then he added politely: "That is very interesting. Good-night, mademoiselle." And making another formal little bow he went out.

Tales of violence of the most dastardly character were spread everywhere in Petrograd and produced, for a while, a mild hysteria in the foreign colonies.

Hysteria always produces ludicrous situations. An Englishman managed to get aboard a crowded car one evening and was obliged to stand on the back platform. He was very nervous and imagined that one neatly dressed little man avoided his eyes. Reaching down for his watch, he found it missing. Just after that the little man got off the car. The Englishman followed quickly and the little man began to run. The Englishman finally caught him in a yard hiding behind a pile of wood. He said in a commanding voice: "Watch! watch!" The little man promptly handed over a watch.

Safe at home the Englishman found his own watch on his dresser where he had carelessly left it in the morning and a strange watch in his pocket. Very much upset by what he had done, he advertised in the papers and in due time the little man appeared. The Englishman began an elaborate apology; but the little man shut him off. "It's quite all right," he said, "what worried me that night was that I was carrying 3000 rubles and I was afraid you would demand those."

The Soviet government tried to do away with many outworn or difficult customs. They paused in the midst of civil war to change the calendar which up until February 7 was thirteen days behind the corresponding dates in all other countries.

And they abolished classes of society, planned people's theatres, reformed the marriage laws and even the spelling.

The old caste system enforced in Russia since the
time of Peter the Great, in the middle of the 18th
century, was never formally annulled until November 25, 1917. The decree reads as follows:

"All classes of society existing up to the present
time in Russia and all divisions of citizens, all class
distinctions and privileges, class organisations and
institutions and also all civil grades are abolished.

"All ranks—nobleman, merchant, peasant; all
titles—prince, count, etc., and denominations of
civil grades (private, state and other councillors)
are abolished and the only denomination established
for all the people of Russia is that of *citizens of the
Russian republic.*"

Lunarcharsky, Minister of Education, is one of
the most picturesque figures in Russia, and for years
has been known as the Poet of the Revolution. He
is an extremely cultured man and could very pos-
sibly have held the same office under any régime.
He does not believe in mixing art and politics. It
was his idea to turn the old palaces into people's
museums, just as they are in France. It was his
idea to organise the Union of Russian Artists.
These artists, made up of all classes, rich and poor,
have charge of the precious art treasures of the nation. They have decreed that no art objects over
twenty-five years of age shall be taken out of the
country.

Lunarcharsky is a fervid Bolshevik, but when he heard that the Kremlin was razed to the ground he took to his bed and resigned his position. He appeared at his post a few days later when he found that it was a false report.

Right in the middle of the fiercest fighting he got out a decree simplifying the spelling, dropping the superfluous letters out of the alphabet. And he established the School of Proletarian Drama. Like mushrooms, overnight almost, dozens of theatres came into being. Plays were given in factories, in barracks. And they chose good plays by the best authors—Gogol, Tolstoi, Shakespeare. . . . There is so much romance in this whole proletarian movement, such magnificent and simple gestures, it is not surprising that it caught the imagination of an impressionable man like Lunarcharsky. Lunarcharsky and Professor Pokrovsky, who holds the chair of history in the University of Moscow, and is another ardent Bolshevik, are both true types of the old intelligentsia who have thrown their lot with the Soviets.

As for the new marriage laws so widely discussed abroad and misunderstood by various indignant and righteous public characters; instance, Mrs. Pankhurst's latest outburst against certain elements in Russia, in which she claimed that women over eighteen have been made public property and proved it by a decree published in a French newspaper. I was present at the meeting when the decree of the Soviets regarding marriage was passed and have the correct data. The decree which fell into the hands of Mrs. Pankhurst was gotten out by persons of absolutely no authority, a little remote group of Anarchists in Odessa. There was no reason at all to get excited about it. Groups of Anarchists all over the world have held strange and outlandish opinions—there are some in America that do, but that doesn't prove theirs is the will of the American people.

According to the marriage laws passed early in January, nothing but civil marriages are recognised. Civil marriages do not mean common law marriages, but those that have been legalised by process of law. All the contracting parties have to do is to go before the Department of Marriage and Divorce and register. No ceremony is necessary. Divorce is equally easy. Either or both of the parties can swear they find it impossible to live together any more, and they are legally free. If there are children the affair is a little more complicated and the one who has the most money, either the man or the woman, must give the most financial aid. The same decree declared all divorces pending in the churches to be null and void.

Declarations of marriage are not accepted from persons of close relationship or those in direct line. No bigamy is allowed. The age at which marriages are legalised in Great Russia is eighteen for the males and sixteen for the females.   In the Trans-Caucasian countries the ages are lowered to sixteen and thirteen respectively.

Just before the vote was taken on this decree one soldier arose and said that he thought the government should limit the divorces to three.   Another soldier got up and denounced him, saying: "Why should we, who believe in freedom, tell any man how many times he should wed?"   So the discussion was dropped.   It is interesting to note that with marriage and divorce as easy to get as a cup of tea there has been no great rush to the bureau. With the removal of all kinds of suppression immorality notably lessens.   Russia with all these lax laws can boast of less immorality than any country in the world.

One of the most puritanical acts of the Bolsheviki was to raid all the gambling houses, to confiscate the money and turn it over to the army and the poor.   They went even further and posted notices giving the names of all persons who frequented these places.

Women's magazines are not popular in Russia, equality of the sexes is too settled a thing.   The only interesting woman's magazine I came across was edited by Madame Samoilova and was contributed to solely by factory women.   It has a circulation of twenty-five thousand.   Children's magazines have reached a high stage of development. They publish one called *Our Magazine*. All the illustrations and stories and poems are the work of small children. Most of the great Russian artists are interested in it and some fascinating numbers have been produced. Civil war and the last German invasions, of course, have temporarily stopped all this delightful spirit of play.

Russians are not very happy away from their own country. Many of the rich Russians, no longer comfortable at home, now seek our shores or go to Sweden or Norway, France or England. But they are not content, they are not at all like the old exiles who fled away from the tyranny of the Tsar. Russia has a strong hold on all of her children. Eventually they will have to go back and work it all out together, as we did in our Civil War, as they did in France. . . .

Pogroms among the Jews have almost ceased. This anti-Semitic feeling, like all race hatred, is artificial and has to be artificially stimulated. With the fall of the monarchy and the discrediting of the reactionaries, the Jews ceased to be segregated according to religion and became Russian citizens. Many of them did excellent work in reorganising. This was especially true of those exiles who had lived a long time in America and had become acquainted with American efficiency. William Shatoff became a member of the famous Military

Revolutionary Committee, organiser of the Printers' Union and a member of the Executive Committee of the Factory Shop Committees. He has lately been reported to be governor of Karkov. Voskoff became head of the Factory Shop Committees at Sestroretz, and was one of the chief inventors of that ingenious institution. Under the old régime one of the chief causes for pogroms was the crowding together of Jews in the Pale so that they were forced in self-defence to combine against the Gentiles. Now there is absolutely no occasion for these hideous performances and none can occur, except those invited by the Black Hundred who are working to put back a Tsar on the throne. The high place and the respect accorded Trotsky give evidence of the real feeling of the people.

Owing to the terrific scarcity of paper in Russia, ordinary postage stamps were used for kopecks, minus the glue. The one ruble notes were pasted together again and again until finally they became very rare. And there was absolutely no metal money. We had to use forty and one hundred ruble notes, and as the merchants had no change we had to establish credits. In the restaurants where we ate most frequently we either gave them the money in advance or they trusted us.

When I read absurd stories of Russia I always am reminded of the experience of the *Evening*

Post's correspondent who was down the Volga, last summer, absorbing atmosphere. He said one afternoon he sat in a one-roomed peasant's hut jotting down impressions. He wrote: "Rough wooden table and benches—large bowl in the centre of the table from which the whole family eats—woman and dirty baby. . . ." But just then he was interrupted, the baby put his feet on the table and the mother scolded it sharply. "Remember you are not in America," she said.

CHAPTER XXIX

A TALK WITH THE ENEMY

ONE often wonders what is working in the German mind. In Russia it was possible for some of us to find out how the common soldiers of Germany and Austria reacted to the terrible tyranny under which they live. Delegates from the two million war prisoners who met in the Foreign Office became so impregnated with Bolshevik propaganda and spread it so thoroughly among their men that whenever a prisoner escaped and got back into Germany he was kept in a detention camp for two weeks and fed on literature gotten out by the German government and calculated as a cure for the revolutionary fever. Every prisoner was forced to undergo this ordeal before he was allowed contact again with his own people. No one realises more than the German officials the effect of working class conscience on their imperialistic aims.

I travelled direct from Petrograd to Stockholm. No greater contrast is possible than to go from a city under the sway of a proletarian dictatorship to a royal city where a king sits in ermine on an ancient throne.

Stockholm buzzes with intrigue. On the mag-

nificent terrace of the Grand Hotel, where fresh
flowers are "planted" beside the fountains every
day, one rubs elbows with people from every corner of the world. The air is heavy with plots and
counter-plots. Spies from the Entente and the
Central Powers dodge round the corners. Guests
speak in subdued tones with their heads close together, glancing furtively from side to side.

I dined there with a diplomat. A tall middle-aged
man passed. My host and the man stared at each
other coldly and my host sighed. "There are things
about the war that are hard to get used to," he said.
"For example, the fellow that just passed is a German. I have known him for years, but I have been
away a long time and only lately returned to Stockholm. A few weeks ago he was lunching here with
friends when I came through with a party—before
we thought what we were doing, we rushed forward
and shook hands. It was extremely embarrassing
and we were both reprimanded. . . ."

Stockholm was overcrowded. It was impossible
to get rooms in any hotel; I appealed to the American legation and they got me into a little pension
on Clarabergsgatan. I wanted to tell the landlady
that I would be leaving the next day, but she spoke
only Swedish. By signs I tried to indicate that
I wanted an interpreter. At last she understood
and after showing me to my room she returned in
a few minutes with an athletic young man who
clicked himself in with a sort of military air and

made a stiff little bow. He spoke English with
scarcely an accent, explaining briefly what I
wanted. When he had finished the landlady smiled
and went out, but the young man stood still in the
middle of the room staring before him. I stirred
the fire and waited for him to go.

Suddenly he came closer. "I am a German," he
announced.

I tried not to appear surprised and there was an
embarrassed silence.

"You are an American," he went on, "so of course
you hate me."

"Let's not talk about it," I answered, turning
away.

"I have to talk about it!" he almost shouted.

Then for the first time I began to observe him
closely. He had a wild look; his eyes were red and
his face drawn as if from lack of sleep. I have
known many soldiers on two fronts and I had seen
them in this state before. He was mentally sick.

"What is the matter?" I asked.

"I have been ordered to go back for the Russian advance."

It was several days before the advance and
I found myself getting excited. "But there is no
Russian advance!" I broke in.

"There will be, I tell you. There will be an advance and I have been ordered back. You must
understand, whether you hate me or not, that I

will not go. I will not fight against the Russian people!"

He paced up and down. "I am in great disgrace," he said miserably. "I have begged to go to the French front, but they will not change their orders. They are stupid and puffed up with victory. They expect me to go into an exhausted country and shoot down a starving population. . . . I cannot do it! German people cannot be so infamous."

"You mean, then," I asked, "that you will openly refuse to fight the Russians?"

"No," he answered in despair. "I will kill myself."

Silence followed. Neither one of us could think of anything to say.

"Liebknecht," I said at last, "is one of the great figures of the war. It is much braver, in my opinion, to do as he has done—to protest against the action of the government than to kill yourself and never be heard of again."

He drew himself up haughtily. "Liebknecht!" he exclaimed in surprise. "Why, he is a Socialist!"

"Nevertheless," I went on calmly, "he has the courage to do the unpopular thing, which is more than any German officer can do."

His face turned crimson. "Mademoiselle," he said gravely, "I shall never forget that you have called Liebknecht braver than any German officer."

A long minute passed. "I shall never forget . . ." he hesitated, "because, perhaps, it is true.

"I have suffered much," he went on. "A month ago I came here to recuperate from a wound and for the first time since the war I have read American papers. I have been thinking about many things and I have thought about Russia. I would fight to the end against England, but I will not go a step against Russia. When we fight England we fight an equal. . . ."

I came back to the subject of America. "What did you get out of American papers?"

"Many lies," he said, "and one great truth."

"And that was——"

"That something is wrong with the policy of the German government." He began to reminisce: "My father is a very rich man. He bought me into a smart cavalry regiment. I believed in the military party. But I am different now. I hate that party. They have made my people a thing of shame. I loathe my rulers; I loathe especially the Crown Prince. But what can I do? I do not believe in your 'brotherhood of man.' I am not comfortable with ragamuffins. . . . There is no place for me. Your President has spoken a great truth. He has said that the German people are not bad. . . . Ah, yes, it is true we are not bad and it is not fine with us. . . ."

"If you should go back," I suggested, "and say

you will not take part in the advance into Russia, what would happen?"

"Only one thing can happen in any case if I go back; I will be shot in twenty-four hours."

I looked at my enemy standing straight and young before me. It was true there was no hope for him. He was already in disgrace. He had expressed himself and there was no recourse. On the other hand, he couldn't imagine joining the revolutionists. He was a lost soul. The only thing left was oblivion in some hotel bedroom. "It is not fine . . ." he murmured again in a half-dazed way as he closed the door and stumbled down the narrow stairs.

CHAPTER XXX

SHOPPING IN GERMANY

"IN Germany you can buy anything for money," was the flat statement of an American woman who had just come from Berlin. We were all sitting around in the music room of the tipsy little *Bergenfjord,* somewhere between Norway and New York. This woman and her son were so healthy and prosperous that we couldn't help wondering how they had managed it in a country where we were pretty certain men were starving. Then some one ventured to ask. And this was her answer.

We felt we were really going to get some information about food speculation and graft so common to all warring countries and began to ply her with questions, but she withdrew into herself and answered so enigmatically that we finally had to abandon her in despair. I give parts of our conversation:

"How did you happen to stay in Germany so long after the war, especially after the United States came in?"

"Well, my husband died and I did not feel like travelling."

"Did you have any trouble getting out?"

"Why should I?"

"You might have observed certain things——"

"They understand I'm not interested in politics; all my life I have not been interested in politics."

"Didn't they examine you or anything?"

"Yes, they did examine me once—it was very embarrassing; they made me take off my clothes. . . ."

"Did they scrub you?"

"Of course not. I never heard of such a thing!"

The deck steward came in and passed around declaration blanks to be filled out before we reached New York Harbour. "I really don't know what to do," complained the lady from Berlin. "I don't know what is in my trunks."

"How's that?"

"My maid packed for me."

We tried a new tack.

"Did you find much suffering in Germany among the women and children? We understood that the infant mortality was very great."

"Oh, I don't believe so. People are very well taken care of. I got plenty of milk for my boy."

"How much did you have to pay?"

"A great deal."

"Is it true that they haven't any fat in Germany?"

"Yes, I paid one hundred and fifty marks for a goose—just to get the fat."

"And you say you always had plenty of food and plenty of bread?"

"Yes, one could always buy everything—*there were ways*. When we found we were leaving we ate every last morsel of all that we had stored up."

"Do you believe there will be a revolution?"

"I'm not interested in politics."

We gave her up and went to the smoking-room, where we found the Kaiser's dentist. Rumour ran around the ship that he had come out of Germany on a special passport signed by the Emperor, and further rumours maintained that he had had nine visits from his majesty within the last few months. Allied passengers walked up and down the deck saying queer things about the doctor. They speculated upon just what action they would have taken in similar circumstances. A mild religious youth burst out with sudden fury that the dentist had missed a great opportunity which he prayed every night to have. "I think he was a dirty coward!" he cried. "It would have been so easy just to let his hand slip. . . ."

There was an interesting group around the table at which we were invited to sit down. Two Americans, one a keen, practical Consul-General from one of the little neutral countries, a general of the United States Army, a Russian Prince, still wearing his title, Bessie Beatty, a San Francisco newspaper woman, myself . . . and the Kaiser's dentist.

We fell into a discussion of food speculation in Russia. Somebody said that it was the same in all countries.

"Even in Germany," remarked the Kaiser's dentist.

From that moment he held our attention.

The doctor was an American. He had lived many years in Germany. His practice was exclusively of the court and the high officers. He was saluted, he said, when he drove about Berlin in his car.

"Doctor," said one of the men, "I hope you *hurt* the Kaiser."

The doctor flushed a little and answered slowly, perhaps out of professional pride. "No-o," he said . . . "I didn't."

We began to talk about food conditions.

"It is always easy to get food if you have money," said the doctor.

"Tell us how you did it over there with all the strict rules and regulations," I said.

"There was a regular system. The porters of the apartment houses were in with the speculators and they kept us in touch. I'll give you an instance:

"One morning the maid came and said to us at breakfast, 'There's a man downstairs who has something to sell.' We told her to send him up. When he came in he showed us a large ham. He said he had gotten off the train before he reached Berlin and walked into the city in order to avoid the

guards. While he was telling us his story the
porter came in and said excitedly that the police
were coming. We hid the ham, and the porter
told the police that the man had gone to the top
floor. We lived on the second. While they were
up there the man escaped."

"How did the police find he was in the building?"

"There was a flower shop right across the street.
Two girls who worked there saw the man come in
with the bundle and reported it to the police. And
it was mighty mean of them," he added, "because
we had often bought flowers in their shop."

"After that we were regular customers of this
man until he suddenly disappeared. I had been
wondering what had become of him, when one day
I was called to the telephone. 'I understand,' said
a voice, 'that you have been trading with a certain
man. . . . Well, . . . we have put him out of
business. We had detectives on his trail and we
know his customers. If you would like some nice
flour we could deliver it to you on Wednesday
afternoon at three o'clock.' I agreed.

"On Wednesday morning I was called up again.
'You had better come for the flour yourself,' said
the person at the other end of the wire. 'Not on
your life,' I answered. 'I know the law. Do you
think I want to get fined?' You see, they have a
law in Germany now that the one who delivers the

goods gets fined—the purchaser merely has his goods confiscated.

"Anyway, at three a wagon drew up with two soldiers and a huge sack containing the flour. Because they were in uniform no one paid the slightest attention to them. The funny part was that they weren't soldiers, but that they wore uniforms over their clothes. It was part of the game.

"After they were gone a girl called and presented a bill. There was no name at the top, only the amount in the middle of a blank page. We paid the bill and distributed the flour from one end of the house to the other in case of a search. We put a lot of it in the attic under some papers and left only a small portion in the bin."

So much for shopping among Germany's well-to-do.

We wanted to know how the poor people managed. The doctor didn't seem to be clear about that. "If they don't get enough to eat—they steal," he summed up with some contempt.

"What makes you think so?" asked Miss Beatty, who has more faith in humanity than the doctor.

"Why, I've seen it myself. There was my little girl. She began to look pinched. I said to my wife, 'I bet her nurse is eating her food.' After that she ate in the dining-room with us and she improved at once."

The General, who has a heart of gold, didn't like the conversation, it began to trouble him. "Look here," he said, "weren't you feeding that girl enough?"

The doctor coloured. "Whoever fed a German servant enough?" he burst out. "They eat like horses."

"Do you think the masses are restless? And that there will be a revolution?"

"I am sure I don't know," he said vaguely. "I didn't keep in touch; in fact, I never talked to them about it."

He assured us that it was true that they had paper clothes which had to be washed a special way or they would dissolve, and the bread, he said, contained no wood, "Because I masticate very well and I never was aware of it."

"And how does your passport read?" one of the company queried.

The doctor smiled.

"It says *'no return'* and I'm perfectly satisfied."

The steward came and turned out the lights and we all filed down the long hallway to bed.

I got up pretty early and went to work. I was in the library, pounding out this story, when the doctor appeared.

"By the way," he began, a little belligerently, "I'd like to speak to you about last night. I shall have to request you not to use anything I said."

"You can hardly do that because you were informed in the beginning that we were newspaper reporters looking for news."

"I don't want my name used," he said.   "I have too many interests in Germany to have them spoiled by anything so trivial."

I promised not to use his name and I don't care to interfere with his interests, but perhaps they will forgive him anyway.   You will remember he said that he didn't hurt the Kaiser.

CHAPTER XXXI

ADVENTURES AS A BOLSHEVIK COURIER

I CAME back from Petrograd as far as Stockholm as a Bolshevik courier. It came about in this way: I was very worried about my papers. Once before when I travelled through Finland most of my baggage was confiscated. I didn't want it to happen again, so I went to Assistant Foreign Minister Zalkind and asked how I could avoid a similar experience. He thought for a moment, smiled and said, "Why, I will make you a courier for the Soviet Government."

I had no idea what it would mean to be taken for a Bolshevik outside of Russia. Dr. Zalkind is a subtle person, sometimes I think that he might have felt that it would be an illuminating experience for a reporter—and it was.

The night before I left I sent my bags over to the foreign office. Three old servants, who had seen many years of service under the Tsar and who still wore the same old uniforms, stood stiffly at attention ready to perform the ceremony. One held a flaming taper, one the long wax sticks and one the official seal which never left his person while he was on duty and which reposed in the great safe at night.

They were very solemn and never changed the expression of their faces as they pasted all over my heretofore insignificant baggage large white cards that proclaimed in black letters that I was about to depart on an *expédition officiel,* treating me with all the deference due an emissary of His Imperial Majesty. Only the soldiers and sailors, shuffling through the building, looked in at the door and grinned broadly.

When the ceremony was over I went in to say good-bye to Zalkind and he gave me courier's papers and a letter to the Bolshevik Minister in Stockholm. "You might tell him what you see on the way, in case it is exciting," he said.

"Do you expect anything to happen?" I asked.

"Well, the Red Guards are still in power, but we are not sure how long they can hold out. Keep your eyes open, anyway."

One has barely time to arrange one's luggage comfortably in the compartment before the train stops at Bjeloostrov, just at the border of Finland. It is only an hour's ride out of Petrograd. Bolshevik troops were everywhere. They examined my passports, counted me a friend and scarcely glanced at my possessions bravely flaunting the enormous red seals of the Workmen's and Peasants' Government.

The trip was uneventful until we reached Tamerfors. Here a company of sailors, who had come to help the Red Guard, were arrested by the White Guard, and sombrely marched away. I regretted that this was my last glimpse of the adventuresome Cronstadt sailors, for they, more than any other group, held our imaginations during the proletarian dictatorship.

My train was the last one allowed to pass. I learned in Stockholm that the Cronstadt sailors had been shot. When the Germans and the White Guards came into power terrible things immediately followed. Seven thousand men and women belonging to the Red Army were slaughtered after they had been disarmed. The German method of killing these poor people was this: They took them in batches of fifty, stood them against a wall and turned on the machine guns. If I had been a few hours later in departing from Petrograd, carrying papers from the Bolsheviki, I would have probably shared their unhappy fate.

At Tornea the American officer had gone away to be married, and a lithe young Cossack had charge. I wasn't sure he was a Bolshevik and hesitated to present my credentials. He began at once to ask me questions in very good English. "Are you just coming from Petrograd? Are you a Socialist?" And before I could answer he went on proudly: "I myself am a Socialist, and I am much interested in the Bolshevik movement. There is great chance for advancement. Look at me! I am under thirty and I am a General. What man in your country is a General under thirty?"

From Tornea to Haparanda everything was frozen, so we rode from one town to the other in a sleigh. The Cossack general accompanied me. He was very happy, telling me all about himself. We were only a few miles from the Arctic circle. He suggested to me that it would be a very nice experience for an American correspondent to walk over. It was not quite three o'clock in the afternoon and the sun, which had been up only a few hours, was already setting, casting back into the sky flames of yellow and gold, reddening the snow. Two little sleighs, drawn by reindeer, in each of which sat a man, came flying from opposite directions. The drivers seemed to have no control of the furious little animals, who dashed at each other, upsetting everything.

We didn't leave Haparanda until about eight in the evening. I had my dinner there and walked through the town, poking around in the little shops and talking to the peasants. Handsome young Swedish officers and Swedish troops in light blue uniforms and high white fur hats were on every street. I wondered, with a little fear in my heart, if they were about to go into Finland and complicate matters even more.

Almost as soon as we left the border ten German officers came on board. They were dressed in all sorts of odds and ends of garments, and if

I hadn't sat at their table for all three meals the next day, I might not have known who they were. It seems that they had established a regular underground system from Finland, which was working especially well since the White Guards were growing in power.

They appeared to have friends all along the way, and when we got to Stockholm one officer was met by his wife and two children. Since the beginning of the war Finnish young men have been fighting in the German trenches against the Russians. It is an undisguised fact, which has been proven by the recent actions of the Finnish government, that the sympathies of the conservative classes in Finland, like the sympathies of the conservative classes in Sweden, are pro-German. Nevertheless, it was rather startling to see such open co-operation.

As soon as I got to Stockholm, I tried to find the Bolshevik officials. I thought maybe a courier would be going back, and I wanted to get word to them about the German officers. My troubles began at once. I went into the largest hotel because I had no definite address, and asked the clerk if he knew where the Bolshevik office was located. He threw me a hostile stare: "Down in some cellar, probably. We have no information about such people."

Curious to see the effect, I continued, "But I am a courier for the new Russian Government."

"We have no rooms in the hotel," he said, turn-

ing his back, which may or may not have been an
answer to my remark.

Next I went to the American legation.   Just
across the court before the entrance I noticed the
old Russian imperial double eagle on a sign bear-
ing the words, "Russian Consulate."   So I went
across the yard and entered the building.   I heard
voices inside, and knocked at the door.   Loud shouts
of "Enter!" summoned me into an ill-lighted room.
In one corner hummed a samovar.   A lot of people
were sitting at a table drinking and eating sandwiches.   Clothes were strewn on chairs, and an
unkempt baby gurgled noisily from the middle of
the floor.   A man came forward and asked me what
I wanted.   I said nonchalantly, "If this is the Bolshevik office, I have a letter and some information
for you."

Immediately everybody jumped up in great excitement, and they all began talking at once as only
Russians can.

"We have nothing to do with Bolsheviki!   We
do not receive their representatives."

"Well, at least," I said, "you could tell me where
they are located."

"We have nothing to do with Bolsheviki!"

I was getting a little weary of being treated in
this fashion by snobbish individuals.

"If you represented the Provisional Government,
or even if you were the representatives of the
Tsar's government, the one thing you would be in-

formed about would be the whereabouts of the new power."

"We have nothing to do with the Bolsheviki!" they cried, screaming with rage and slamming the door.

I started back to the legation, and met a correspondent from one of our biggest press agencies. I began to feel relieved; I was so sure I would get the right information.

"Will you tell me," I said, as politely as I knew how, "where I can find the Bolshevik headquarters?"

To my utter astonishment he purpled with indignation. "I have nothing to do with such scum!" he answered icily.

I felt myself forced to ask one more question. "If you had to choose between the Bolsheviki and the Germans, which would you prefer?"

Without hesitating he replied, "The Germans."

"Have you ever been in Russia?"

"No."

There was nothing further to say. I went into the American Minister's office and got the right address. It was only a block away. All the people I had asked must have known where it was. I wondered as I went along what sort of terrible folk I would find there. A very slight, almost timid, youth answered my ring. He said the Consul would see me in a minute, and gave me a book and a chair by the fire.

The Consul, Vorovsky, proved to be a well-known musician and a cultured gentleman.   His assistant was a doctor of philosophy, whose imagination had been caught by the romance and the daring of the Bolshevik movement.

"You must be very tired," said the doctor of philosophy, "after your long journey.   Just down the street is a quiet little tea shop where they have nice concerts and the most delicious Swedish pastries.   We will go there and talk."

Seated at the table, we looked out across the wide street at the slow-moving barges going up and down the canals.   Vast Russia lay far behind.   I was homesick for my own country, but I thought of the German advance and my heart ached.   I wanted to go back and offer my life for the revolution.   My companion interrupted my thoughts.

"If you care for Swedish art," he began, "there is an interesting exhibition of Zorn at the National gallery. . . ."

THE END